Conker Editions Ltd
22 Cosby Road
Littlethorpe
Leicester
LE19 2HF
Email: books@conkereditions.co.uk
Website: www.conkereditions.co.uk
First published by Conker Editions Ltd 2022.
Text © 2022 Gavin Haigh.
Gavin Haigh has asserted his rights in accordance with the Copyright, Designs and Patents Act 1988 to be identified as the author of this work. All rights reserved. No part of this publication may be reproduced, stored in a retrieval system, or transmitted in any form or by any means, electronic, mechanical, photocopying, recording or otherwise, without the prior permission in writing of the publisher and the copyright owners, or as expressly permitted by law, or under terms agreed with the appropriate reprographics rights organisation. Enquiries concerning reproduction outside the terms stated here should be sent to the publishers at the UK address printed on this page.
The publisher makes no representation, express or implied, with regard to the accuracy of the information contained in this book and cannot accept any legal responsibility for any errors or omissions that may be made.
A CIP catalogue record for this book is available from the British Library.
13-digit ISBN: 9781739770518.
Design and typesetting by Gary Silke.
Printed in the UK by Mixam.

BLACK AND WHITE STRIPES
THE GREATEST COLLECTION OF NEWCASTLE UNITED MATCHWORN SHIRTS

GAVIN HAIGH

This book is dedicated to the memory of my parents – to my late father, Bill Haigh, with whom I stood and sat side by side at St James' Park for 32 years, and to my wonderful late mother, Dorothy, who was such a loving support to me with my football shirt interest, from that first visit to the sports shop back in June 1976. I love and miss you both, thank you. x

Foreword

When I was at Leicester City, I first found out from the club that Newcastle had asked whether I was available. As always, I phoned up my uncle for help and guidance.

"You'd be mad not to go to Newcastle," Uncle Ronnie said. "Because if you become a number nine that's a *real* number nine, you'll be remembered forever." Those were his words, before we decided to sign.

The Newcastle United number nine shirt is one of the most iconic in British football. I'll always remember how it felt to pull it on for the first time. There's a real weight of expectation, knowing that fans are comparing you to players like Jackie Milburn, Malcolm Macdonald...

I still go up to Newcastle at least once a year. My son is a Newcastle fan, so he always wants to go to the games. You get a warm welcome from the club and from everybody at St James's.

I collected a vast array of shirts throughout my domestic and international career. I had shirts from Chile, Holland, Germany, Lithuania, Russia – but I received a very handsome figure for most of them a few years back. It's much better for someone to have them and enjoy them than keeping them stored away.

That's why I think Gavin's book is such a super idea, because football shirts mean so much to so many people. They've always been very iconic, very special to me.

The only matchworn ones I have left now are a couple of Ireland shirts and, of course, the Newcastle number nine shirt from my time with the club.

I was wearing it against Portsmouth, at the end of the '91/92 season. We were in the bottom three, and if we'd lost we'd have been relegated to the Third Division. And I scored with about seven or eight minutes to go, arguably the most important goal of my career. It was funny because there came that point when you feel you're going to score. We weren't going to

draw – we were going to win. I just got it into my head. And ultimately I scored, and we survived. And then the whole city exploded!

See the shirt and it takes you back to the match, the era, the atmosphere...

David Kelly

Introduction

My Newcastle United collection and my obsession with football shirts started a few months before I went to my first ever NUFC match, a 3-2 win at home to Birmingham City on 23rd October 1976.

It was in the June that year, having just returned from my first ever holiday abroad in Majorca, that my late mother took the seven-year-old me to Stan Seymour's sports shop in Newcastle to acquire the full home NUFC strip.

I remember wandering around the sports shop, standing at the counter, trying on the strip and watching it being put into a bag whilst my mother paid for it. I was made up immediately. The vivid memories that strip brings back to me are very emotional to this day. I still love that shirt – the black and white stripes, the city crest, the collar with the 'V' inset – as well as the

shorts and the hooped socks. Months later, I even had a red number seven sewn on the back. On returning home, just over the Tyne Bridge to Deckham in Gateshead, I posed for the camera in my new NUFC strip, complete with new football, too.

From that moment, my Newcastle United shirt collection and obsession began. Now it became my objective that every time a new NUFC shirt came out, I had to get it!

Now, 46 years later, that objective continues to be fulfilled, and I own a version of every single replica shirt NUFC have issued since 1968, including home, away and third shirts.

By the late 1980s, my obsession had expanded to matchworn shirts; but, at the time, it was impossible to get a hold of one. I put articles in the NUFC match programme and in football magazines, even reaching out to European titles, and wrote directly to the club a number of times asking for help – all without success.

My first NUFC matchworn shirt breakthrough came in 1991 after my mother wrote to the club. She explained how I was a massive fan, and expressed her disappointment that they weren't offering to help with my quest. Shortly afterwards, the commercial manager contacted her and then visited our home, and having complimented me on my NUFC replica shirt collection, invited me to the next match. After the game, he presented me with a number nine

8

players' shirt! It was one of the very set worn by the reserve team throughout the 1990/91 season.

Some time in late 1991 I learned that my Uncle Billy had a NUFC player shirt that he had received off Mick Quinn. And, as my mother was going to visit him in the USA in the summer, she would ask him if she could bring it home for me. You can imagine my joy when she presented it to me on her return. I can't begin to say how grateful I am to them both for this shirt.

In 1997 I entered a competition in the *Black and White* magazine to win Robbie Elliott's shirt from when we beat Nottingham Forest 5-0 to qualify for the Champions League. Of course, Robbie scored that day. And, amazingly, I won the shirt!

These are fantastic memories from the 1990s. I'd finally obtained some NUFC matchworn shirts after so many years of trying.

Heading into the new millennium, I was at last introduced to eBay, to online auctions and football shirt websites, which brought new opportunities and some immediate success.

My NUFC matchworn collection has since expanded so much that the time has now come to share some of it with fellow fans and collectors.

Sadly, there wasn't room to include all my shirts here, leaving me with the task of curating a selection with the most significance, both personal and historical. A tough call, as I've currently amassed 275 matchworn/player shirts, including a player-worn example of every home, away and third shirt from 1976 to date. Along with all the replica shirts I also own, the NUFC collection sits at close to 1000 – and counting.

I'm very grateful to many football shirt collectors, several of whom have become trusted and loyal friends over

the years, who have been a massive help in making my collection what it is today. I would also like to thank several NUFC players, past and present, for their support.

I hope you enjoy *Black and White Stripes*.

HWTL – Gavin Haigh, August 2022

1 UNNUMBERED

1957-59 - Floodlights Shirt

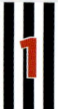

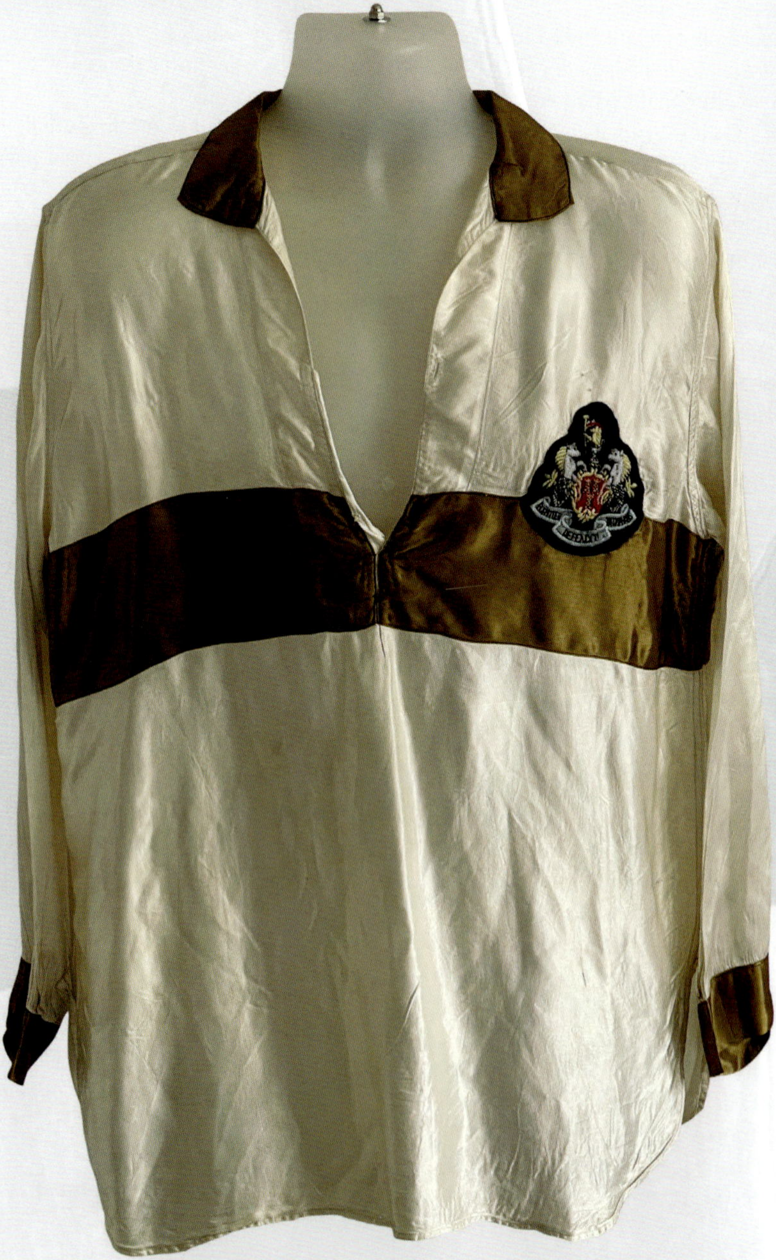

The city's coat of arms first appeared on Newcastle United shirts in the 1910 FA Cup final. A slightly different version was worn in the final a year later – and then in each of our subsequent eight Cup finals – but the club crest didn't appear in Football League matches until as late as 1969/70.

The 14th-century coat of arms shows a version of Newcastle's history, with the Norman castle and seahorses to represent the city's maritime tradition. *Fortiter Defendit Triumphans* means 'Triumphing by Brave Defence', a reference to an historic battle against the Scots rather than to the team's Edwardian back line.

This treasured Bukta shirt design was a special one-off made from shiny, silky material that implies use under floodlights. Indeed, the excellent HistoricalKits.co.uk tells us NUFC played a number of floodlit friendlies in the winter of 1957. Only black-and-white photos survive, showing a light strip was worn with a contrasting, reflective dark band, in just this style. Similar photos suggest this was also the kit worn in Norman Smith's 1959 testimonial match.

2 ALAN FOGGON

1968/69 - Fairs Cup

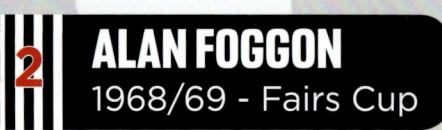

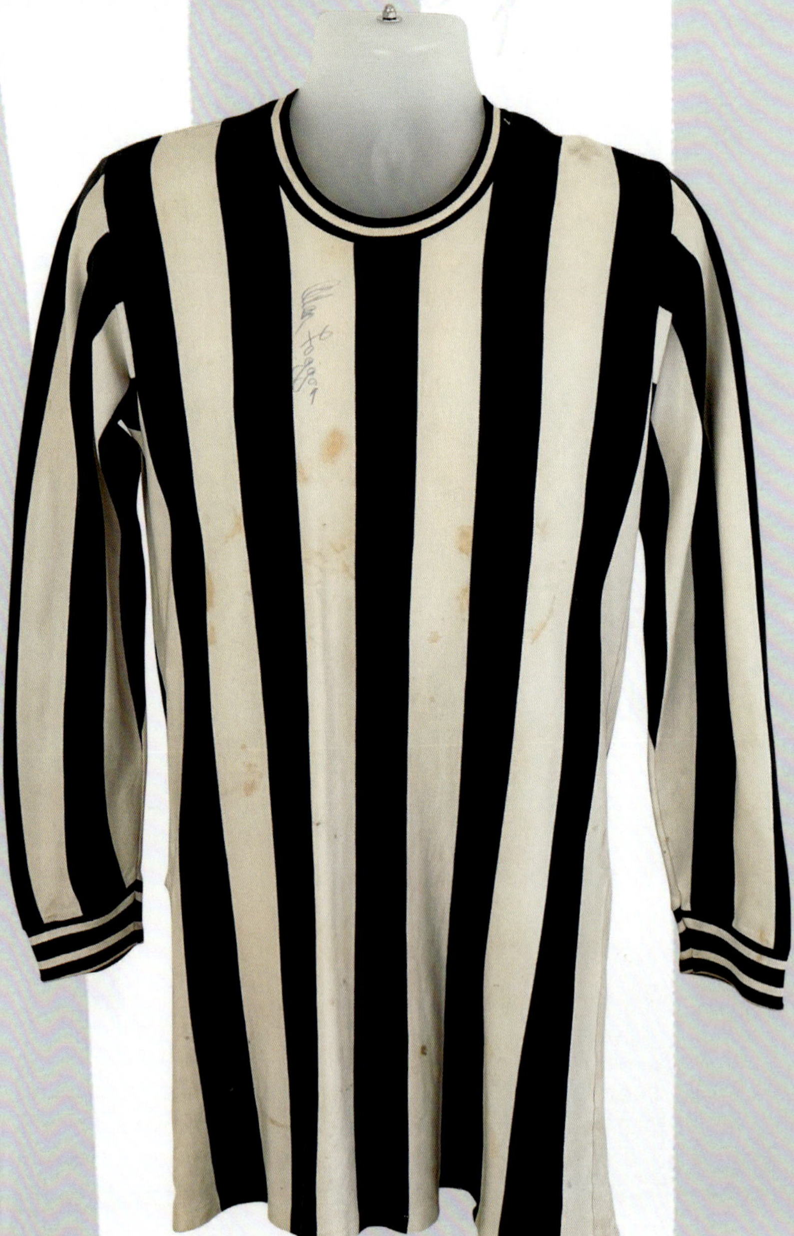

A very well-worn matchworn number 12 shirt from the victorious Fairs Cup campaign.

I bought this shirt from a fellow fan who had inherited it from his late father, it having been in the family's possession for years. He told me that the shirt originally came from the coach driver who, back in the late '60s, had carried the players back and forth from a local hotel on match days. He added that NUFC's local Durham forward Alan Foggon had signed the shirt and given it to him.

A friend of mine asked Alan to confirm the provenance of this signing; unfortunately, he wasn't able to do so, but to be fair it was over 53 years ago!

Nevertheless, this is a remarkable shirt, in that the cotton material is extremely heavy in comparison to more modern nylon designs. The shirt features a number 12 stitched on to a rear panel, and also has a number '100' stamped on the inside collar, which only appeared on player-issue shirts.

3 TERRY HIBBITT
1971/72 - Division One

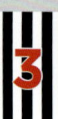

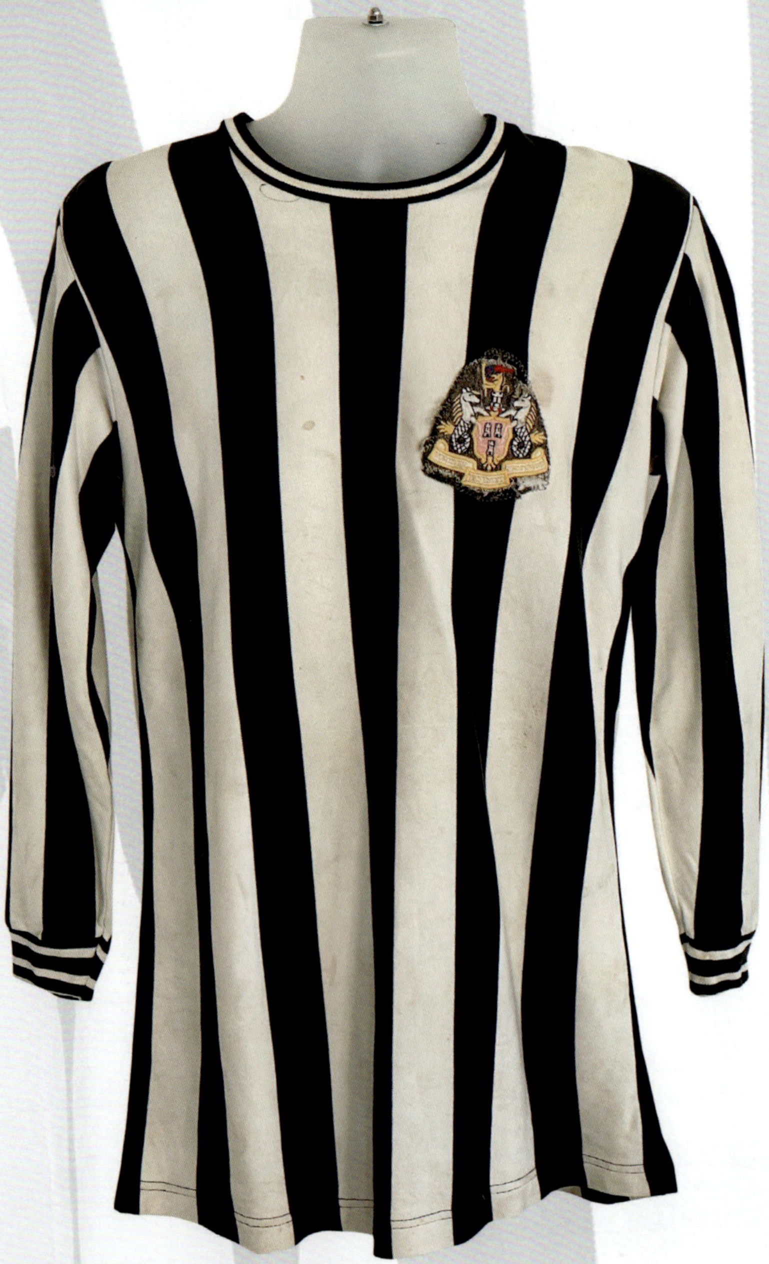

This extremely rare and very heavy number eleven home shirt was worn by Terry Hibbitt over the 1971/72 season, when it honestly must have weighed down the skilful Yorkshire winger, given Terry's small stature. The crest on a shaped patch was a cracking addition to the previous plain black and white striped shirts, with the stitched patch and red numbering unchanged on the back. Hibbitt wore number eleven in every game bar a handful, when Alex Reid and others got a brief look-in.

In the summer of 1971 Newcastle had brought in Malcolm Macdonald from Luton to score the goals, and Hibbitt from Leeds to act as his supply line. Who can forget the pair's home debut, when we beat Liverpool 3-2 and Supermac scored a hat-trick?

Hibbitt made 259 appearances, scoring 13 goals across two great spells – from 1971 to '75, when he was sold to Birmingham City, and then from April 1978 up until his retirement in the summer of '81.

Personal memories of him include the famous terrace chant at the match: "Terry, Terry Hibbitt, Terry Hibbitt on the wing…"

4

BOB MONCUR

1973/74 - Division One

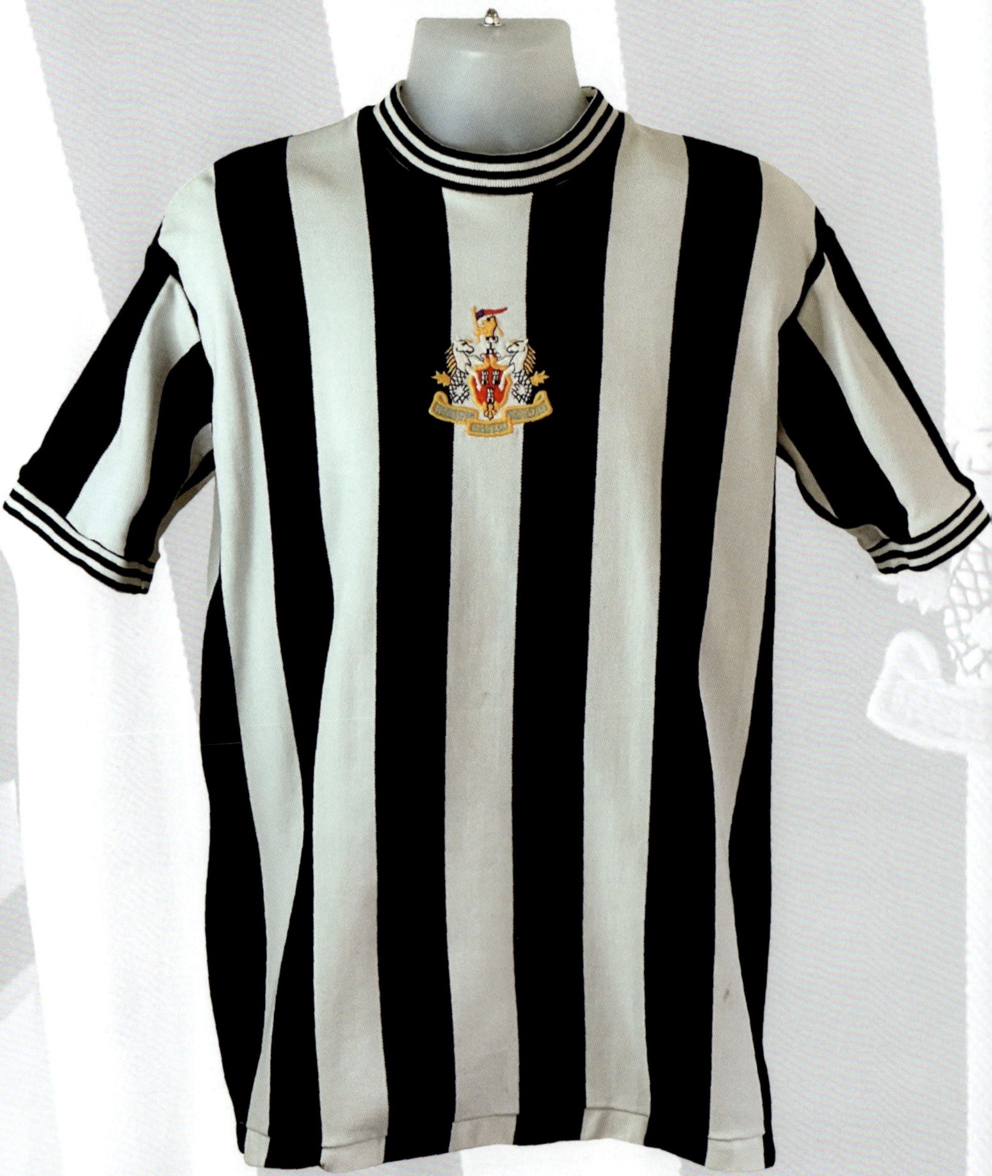

the shirts were then sent to the club where the city-crest badge was stitched on along with the rear patch and red number.

In the days before visible shirt branding, sponsorship deals and commercialisation, the fact that

This matchworn number six shirt was worn throughout the 1973/74 season by longtime skipper and club legend Bob Moncur, who made a total of 360 appearances for the Magpies between 1962 and '74.

The Admiral Soccerstyles catalogue of 1974 featured these 'Authenticolour' jerseys, 'generously cut in 100 per cent nylon airflow stretch fabric', which were supplied to many Football League clubs, including Newcastle United.

Once manufactured by Admiral,

Admiral were producing the shirts worn by Newcastle United was not widely known at the time. Even today, this information has so far escaped the attention of many football shirt aficionados and specialist websites.

Even in retrospect, when you're well aware of Newcastle United's proud footballing history, it still seems incredible that our appearance in the 93rd FA Cup final was our eleventh – then a record for any club. Liverpool, meanwhile, were mere beginners, making only their fifth appearance. Add it up: in all the years the final had been held since 1872, on average we'd been involved in English football's biggest occasion once every eight-and-a-half years.

Unfortunately, that record was probably the highlight of the day, as the lads were comprehensively outplayed by the Reds, going down to three second-half goals.

Tommy Cassidy's matchworn number eight shirt from the game shows the special one-off feature used on the day, a stylised buck logo above the 'Bukta' embroidery.

Like all of our players, the Northern Ireland international midfielder chose a short-sleeved shirt for the final. Also, it is believed that two NUFC fans that day were the first to wear replica shirts at a British game, having squeezed into junior sizes!

6

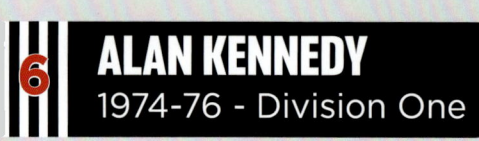

ALAN KENNEDY

1974-76 - Division One

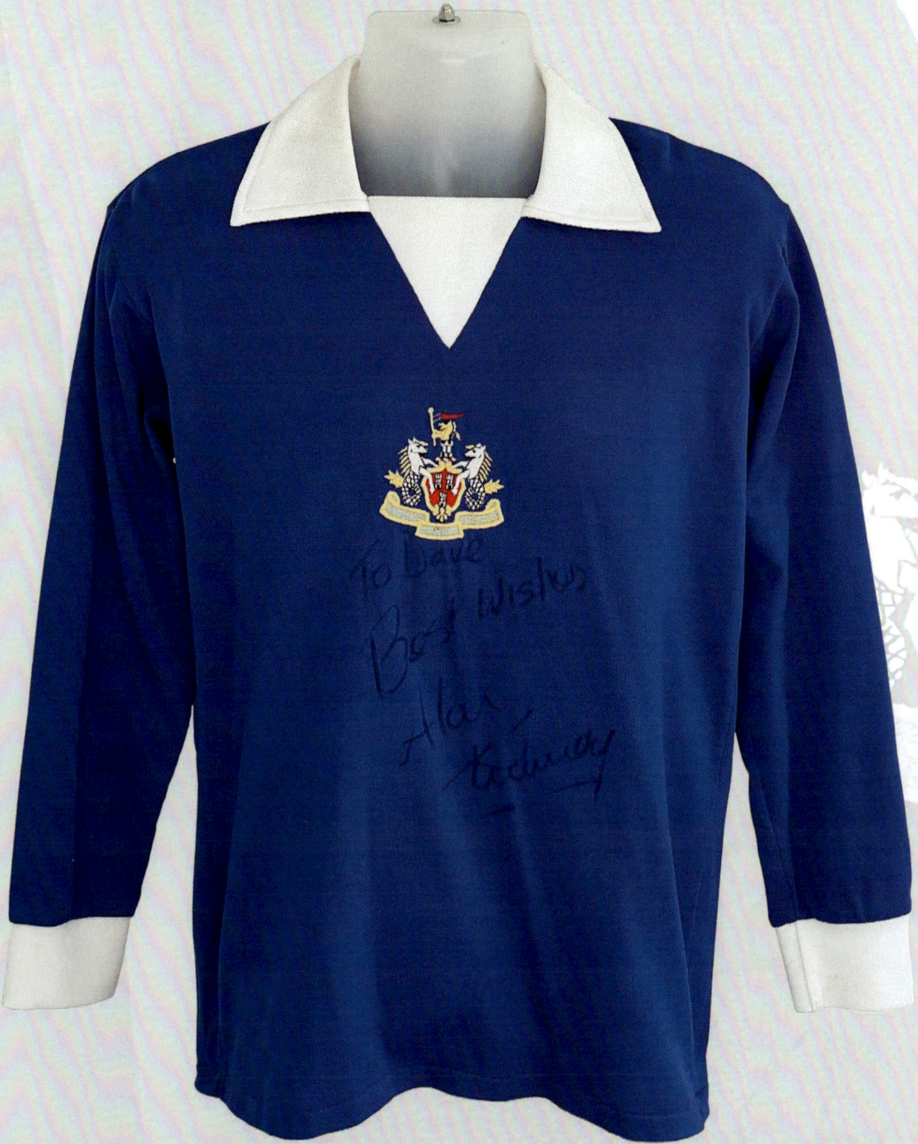

the shirt at a Fairs Club event. He confirmed he wore the number eight during a brief foray into midfield in late 1974, also recalling that it was very uncomfortable to wear out on the pitch!

Only rarely did Newcastle United take to the field in blue shirts in this era (worn with blue shorts with white trim, and blue and

Here's an incredibly rare matchworn blue number eight away shirt, fashioned from 100 per cent nylon.

Once again, it is an example of classic Admiral teamwear from the early/mid '70s. The blue shirts, designed with white collars and 'V' insets, were produced by the Leicester manufacturer and subsequently hand-finished with crest and number at the club.

I recently talked to Alan Kennedy about

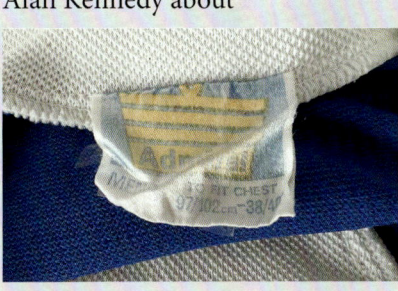

white hooped socks), although TV footage does exist of an otherwise forgettable 5-0 defeat at Wolves in 1976 – which alone proves that the shirts were in use by the first team over a two-year period.

7

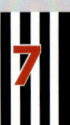

MICKY BURNS

1975 - Anglo Scottish Cup

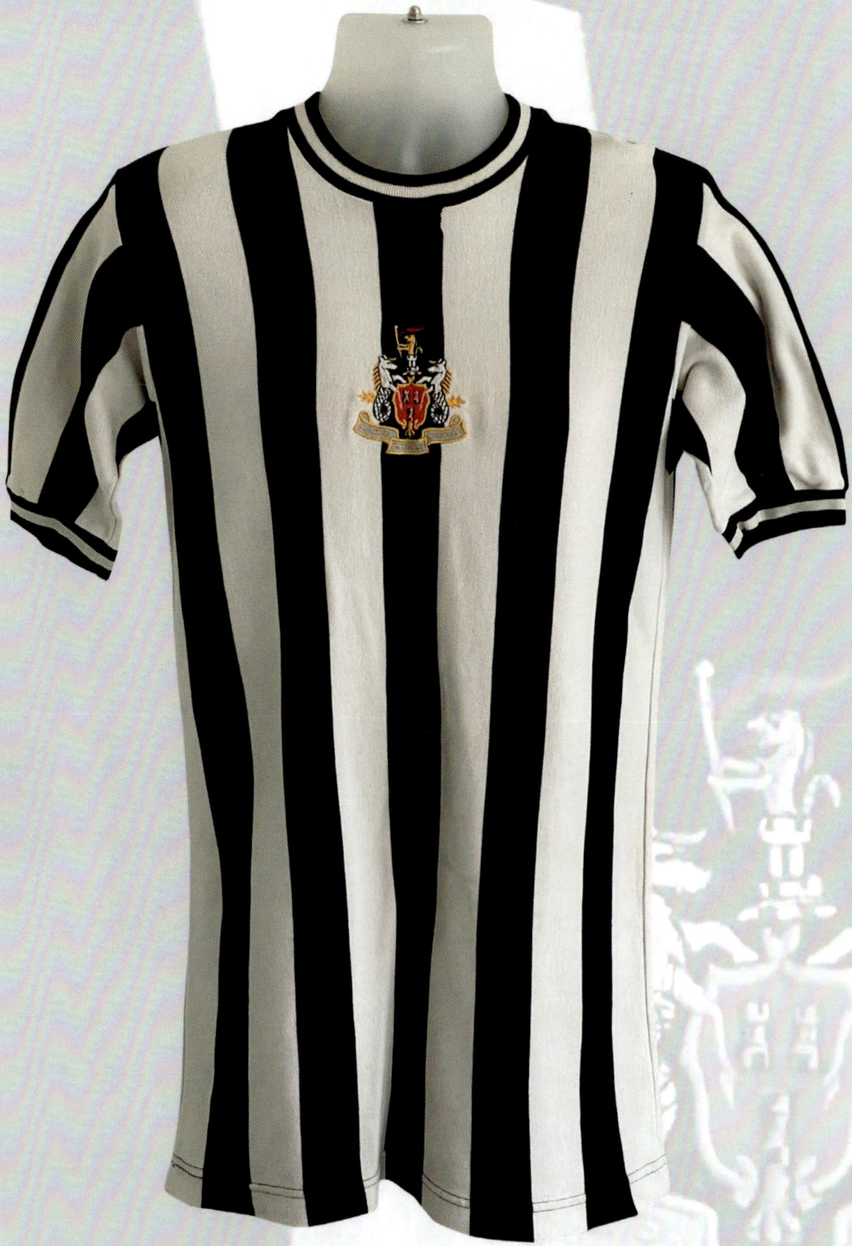

stripe on collar and cuffs, and the number seven was clearly sewn on by hand as opposed to being machine stitched.

Maybe the club had yet to take delivery of the new-style shirts, as the big Division One kick-off at Ipswich was still a week away

Look it up on YouTube and you can see vintage TV footage of this shirt in action for the Magpies against Middlesbrough on 9th August 1975. This pre-season fixture was an Anglo-Scottish Cup tie, and ended in a 2-2 draw. It's worth noting that our only other opponents in this mysteriously short-lived competition were not Rangers or Celtic but Carlisle United and the Mackems.

Far more worthy of note than the international club trophy at stake in these pre-season friendlies is the shirt itself. In the 1975/76 season the home shirts used in Football League matches were equipped with black collars and 'V' insets, so it would appear that the previous season's shirts with the round necks were worn in games such as this one. This shirt has a single – closely followed by the League opener at St James' Park, a rematch against Boro which ended up another score draw, one apiece.

8

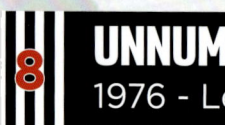

UNNUMBERED

1976 - League Cup Final

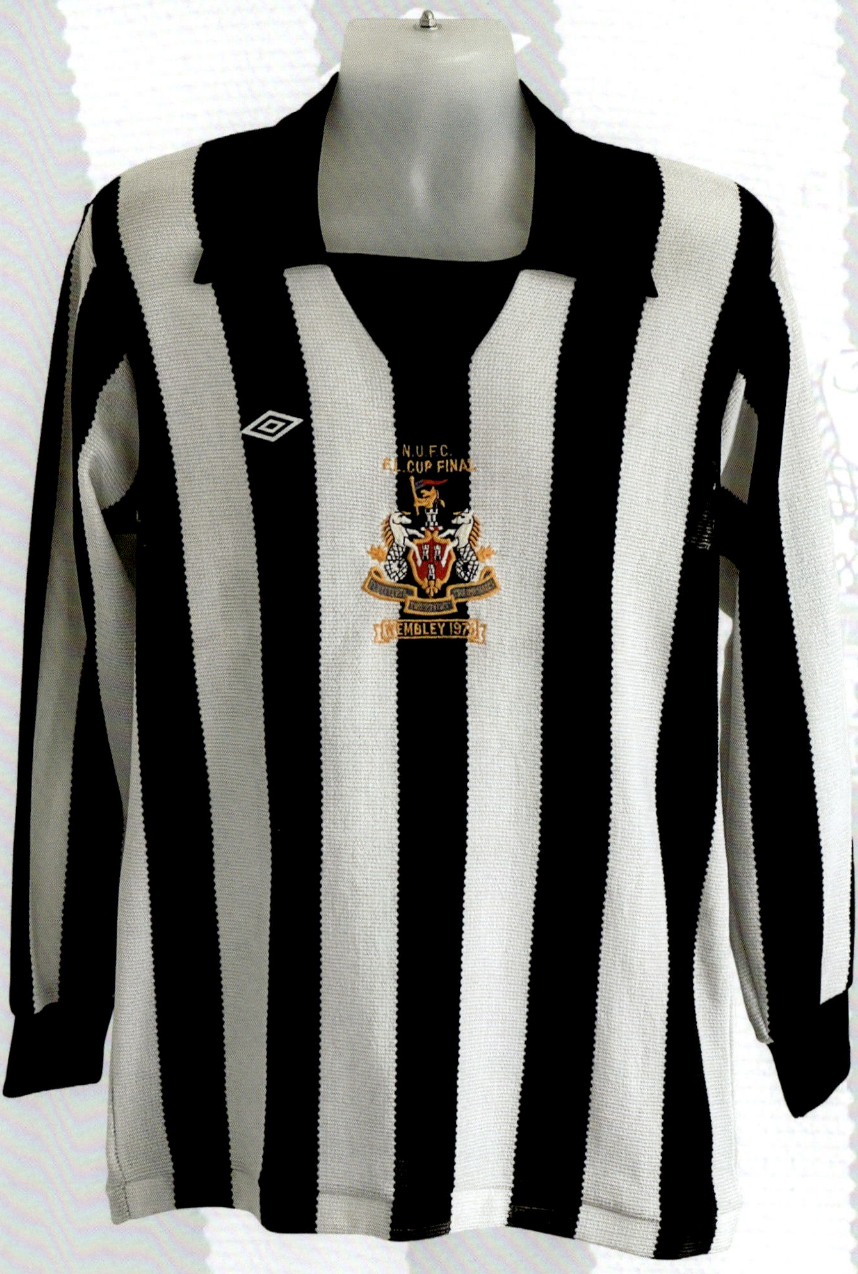

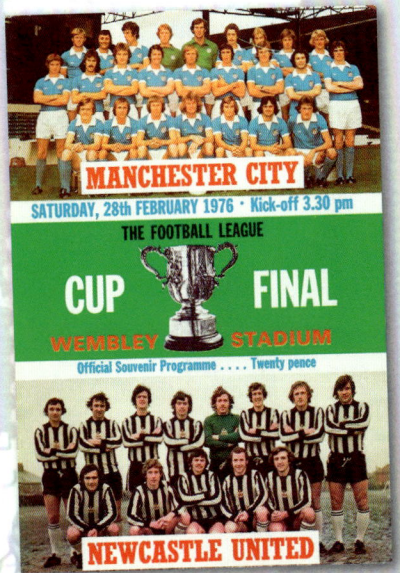

special League Cup final lettering.

Sadly, we lost the final 2-1 after Alan Gowling had equalised Peter Barnes' opener for City, the winning goal then coming from Dennis Tueart's overhead kick.

So near, yet so far...

Tantalisingly, I visited Alan at his house in late 2016, when he showed me the full number ten strip that he wore on the day. A

Match issued for the League Cup final against Manchester City on 28th February 1976, this shirt remained unnumbered and was not ultimately used at Wembley Stadium.

Major features of the Umbro-produced shirt, equipped with black collars and 'V' inset, include the extra-thick, jumper-like material and the embroidered badge with

year earlier, on a Fairs Club trip, Pat Howard had also shown me his worn number six shirt from the game. Hopefully, one day, I will secure an actual matchworn, numbered shirt for the collection.

NUMBER TEN
1976-78 - Division One

George Robledo and his brother Ted were footballing pioneers, not only the first South Americans to play for Newcastle (between 1949 and 1953), but also the first to play as pros in England. In 1951/52, George won the Golden Boot with 33 goals, the first top scorer from overseas, and also scored the winning goal in the 1952 Cup final, overall making 166 appearances and scoring 91 goals.

In 1981 George was invited by NUFC to the 30th anniversary celebration of the 1951 FA Cup win, when he met up with Jackie Milburn, with whom he formed a formidable front pairing in the early 1950s. The club gave George this Bukta number ten shirt as a gift, matchworn by Alan Gowling, Mark McGhee and Terry Hibbitt between 1976 and 1978.

The shirt came into my collection through my friendship with George's daughter Elizabeth, having been connected through Chilean collector Fidel Valenzuela. She wanted to ensure that some of his items, which her father and she treasured, would go to a good home. I am truly honoured to own this shirt, and am so grateful to Elizabeth for the opportunity.

10

STEWART BARROWCLOUGH

1976/77 - Division One

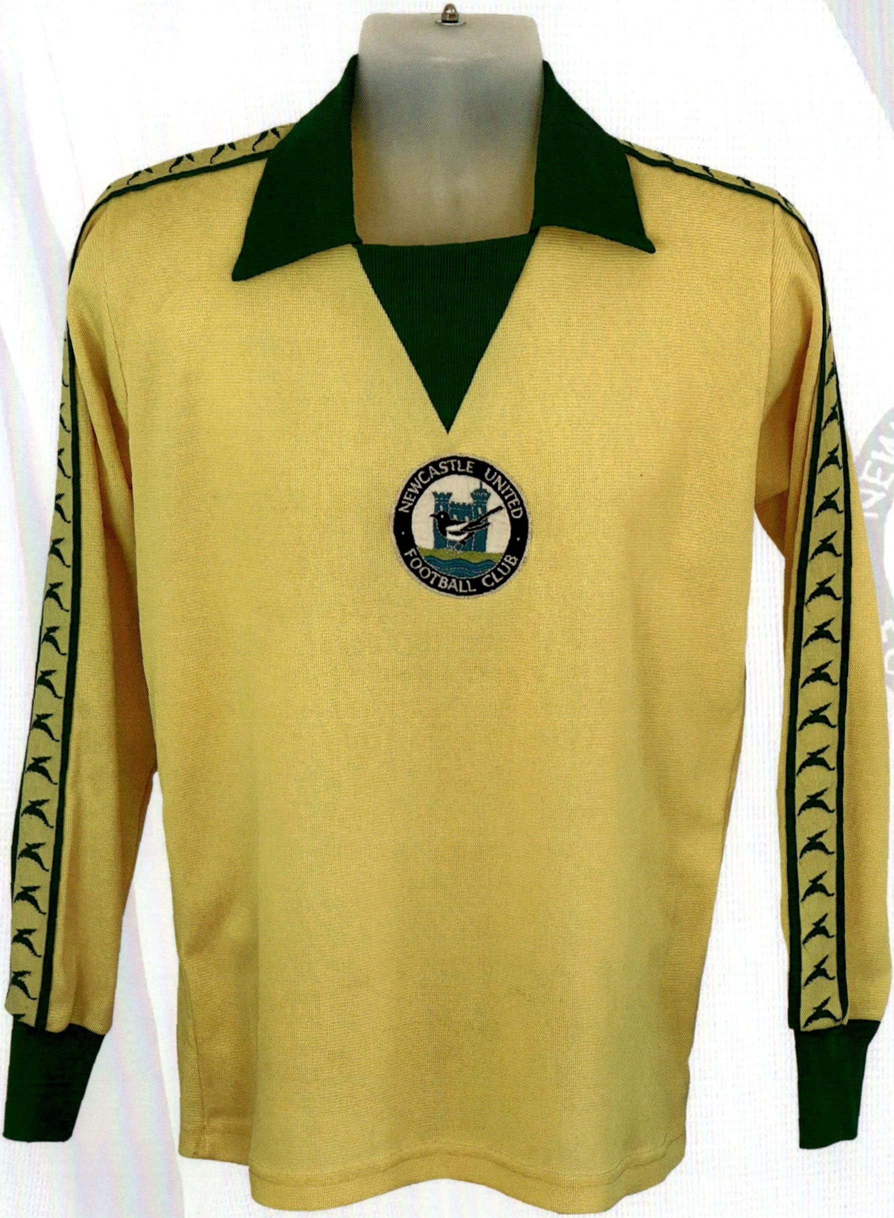

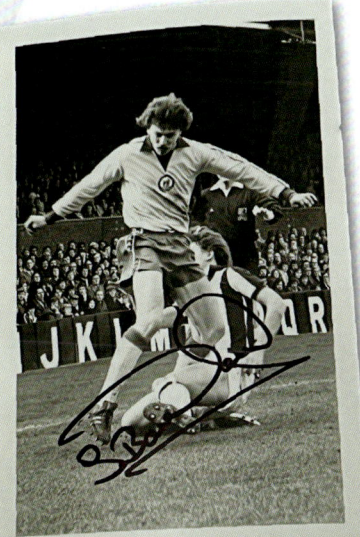

to appear on kits. In the latter part of the decade Bukta followed the general trend of logos down the shirt sleeves and shorts.

This number seven shirt was worn throughout the 1976/77 season by Stewart Barrowclough, who I spoke to recently at a Fairs Club event. Stewart commented that the shirts were very itchy, and also added that players were not allowed to keep a shirt unless

Bukta are the longest-established football apparel manufacturers in Britain, and therefore the world, according to football-kit historian John Devlin. The brand was created by Edward Buck & Sons way back in 1879.

In the days before visible branding, they kitted out many football clubs for much of the 20th century, and in the '60s supplied more Football League clubs than any other manufacturer, as well as the world-beating England team.

It wasn't until the mid '70s that the little stylised buck logo began

it was a Cup final shirt they had worn, this because the shirts were individually sponsored. The club always held a tight rein on kit!

11

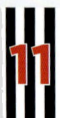

TERRY HIBBITT

1978-80 - Division Two

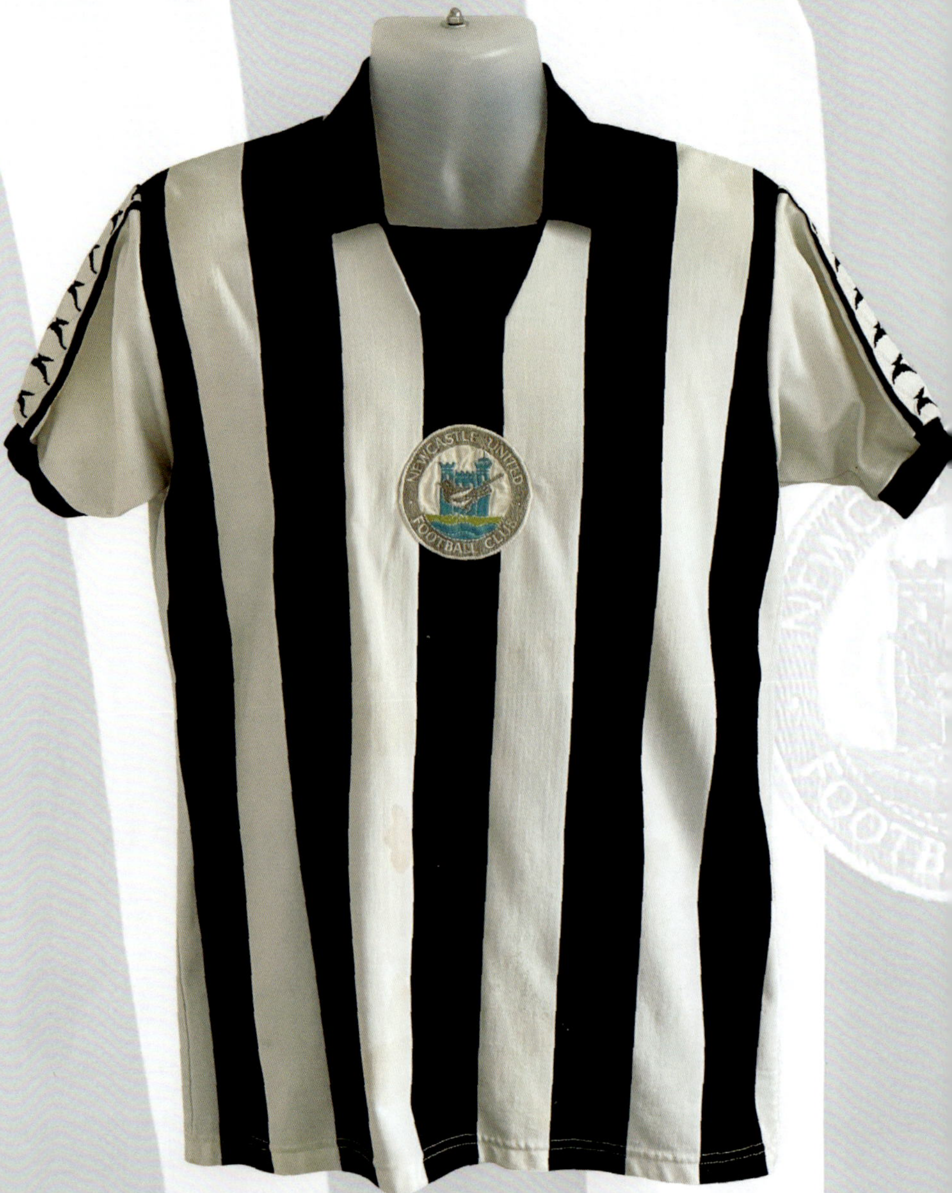

The material on this Bukta shirt was physically different to the one worn from 1976-78. These stripes were slightly thinner, the material was thicker and heavier, and the crest badge appeared faded on a number of shirts, no doubt due

The number ten shirt that was worn mostly by Terry Hibbitt over the two seasons the design was in use: 1978/79 and 1979/80. Billy Rafferty also wore it a dozen times, and Alex Cropley twice.

It featured the first crest designed specifically for the club (first used back in 1976), which featured the city-centre landmark of Castle Keep, a representation of the River Tyne and a magpie. The crest stayed in use until 1983.

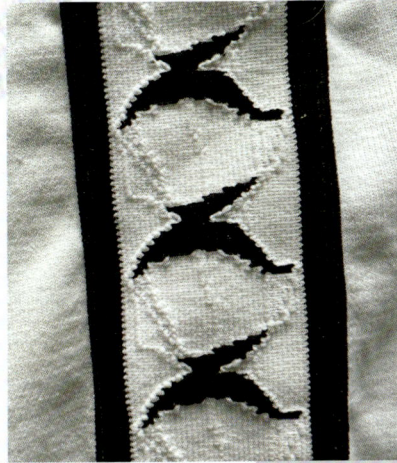

to the numerous washes they had been through over two seasons.

The 1979/80 season saw Newcastle top of Division Two on New Year's Day after a resounding win over Sunderland, but the lads faded away badly during the remainder of the season to finish in ninth place.

12

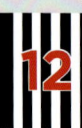

NUMBER FIVE

1978/79 - Division Two

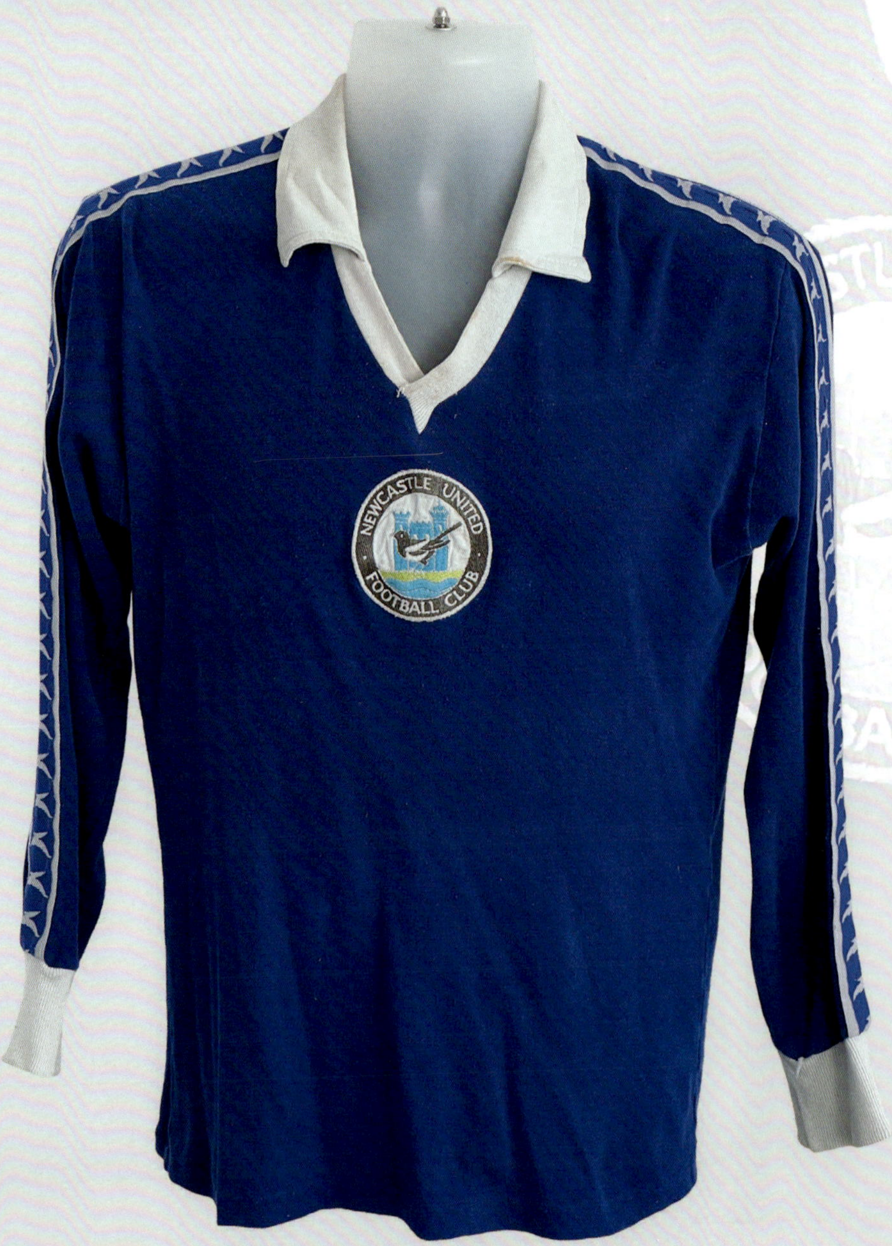

The Bukta number five away/third shirt that was worn against Sunderland at Roker Park on 14th October 1978, a game that ended in a 1-1 draw.

Although I was lucky enough to secure this shirt from David Barton, TV footage and player records indicate that he actually wore number four in this match, while John Bird wore the number five...

I met David through the Fairs Club in 2015 at Stan Anderson's birthday party. Talking about his time at the club, he told me that he was still in possession of this rare blue shirt, and the story of how he came to get it – simply by picking it up off the floor of the dressing-room (where, perhaps inevitably, he was known to teammates as 'Dick' Barton) after the match in question.

We went on to discuss my shirt collection, and David was so impressed he said he'd donate the shirt to the cause. A week later he brought it to my home to present it to me, and even apologised for the condition of the shirt, which he'd been using to jog in. Needless to say, that didn't bother me one iota!

David played 110 matches for NUFC over six seasons to 1983. Meanwhile, John Bird, his partner in defence, played 93 games up until 1980, before becoming an accomplished artist with his own studio and art gallery in Bawtry. I visited him there in January 2017, and had a great discussion about his time in football.

13

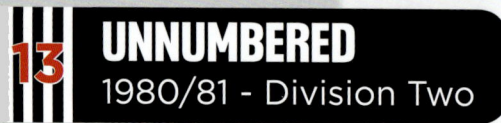

UNNUMBERED

1980/81 - Division Two

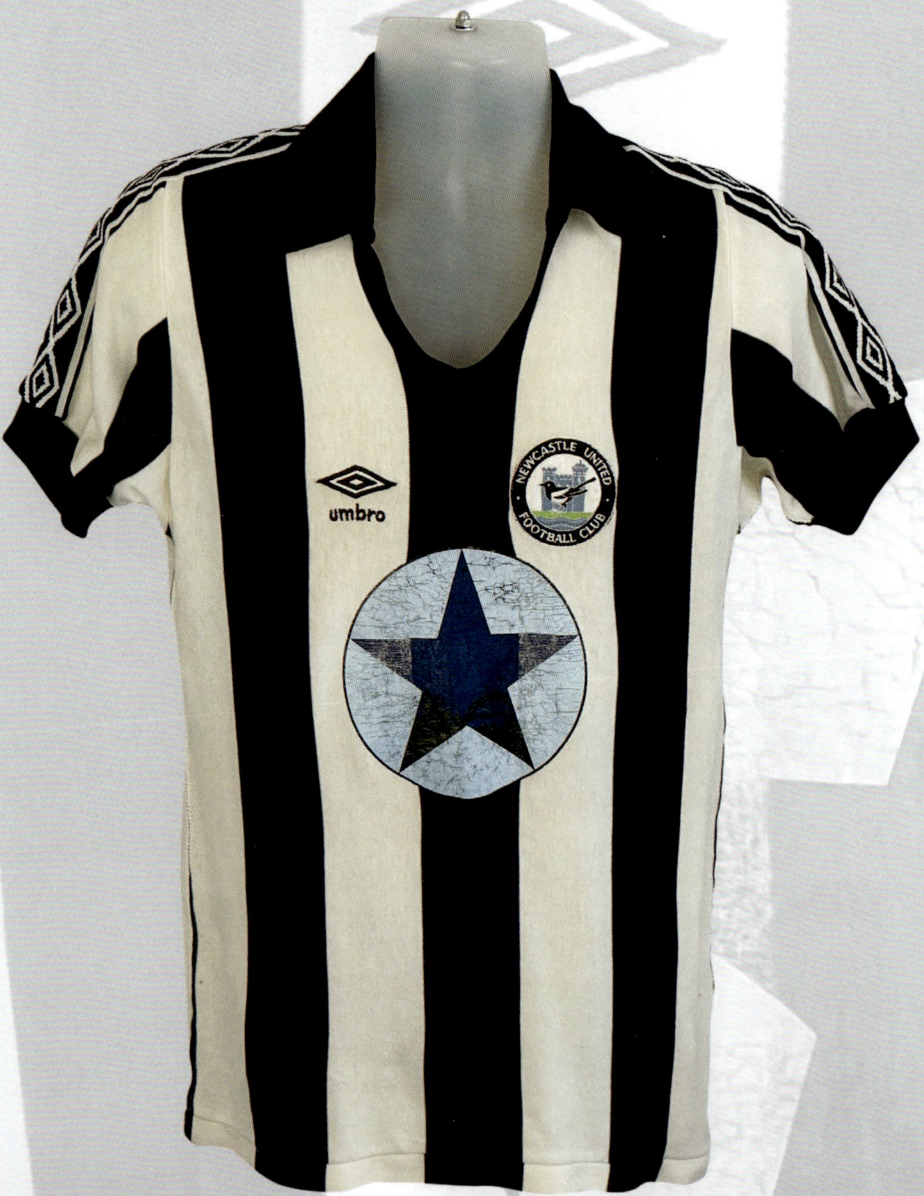

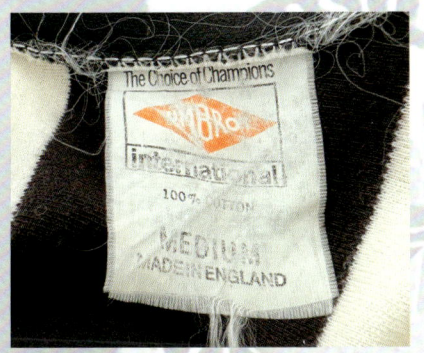

Newcastle Brown Ale logo was a a relatively stylish and inoffensive addition with such strong local roots, and no messy words cluttering up the front of the shirt.

The blue star logo features a silhouette of the city skyline, the

Just one year after Liverpool made history, raking in £50,000 from Hitachi for becoming the first English Football League club to feature a sponsor's name on their shirts, Newcastle United also chose to follow this money-making path.

Quite fittingly, it was Scottish & Newcastle Breweries that became NUFC's first ever shirt sponsor. Compared to other clubs, the

five points of the star representing the five breweries that merged to form Newcastle Breweries in the Victorian era.

This unnumbered player's shirt from 1980 was given to me by a Dutch collector friend, Jesse Rabbeljee.

NUMBER ONE
1980-82 - Division Two

For much of the 20th century, goalkeepers all wore plain green jerseys and the same shorts and socks as their teammates, according to Rob 'Glove Story' Stokes...

Football League laws stated that keeper shirts had to be self-coloured; but by the '70s branding began to creep in along with bespoke shirt design, and the early '80s saw yet more design elements appearing. Then restrictions were withdrawn – and anything went!

This matchworn Umbro shirt from 1980 shows the regulation solid-colour offering with the flappy collar that Newcastle chose for the shotstoppers.

At the time, unsponsored shirts like this one were worn exclusively in televised matches throughout the season – this one diving into puddles in the SJP mud courtesy of Steve Hardwick and Kevin Carr.

NUMBER 18
1980-83 - Division Two

was damaged in a match. When QPR played at St James' Park in May 1982, an unforeseen kit clash – our home stripes vs their home hoops – saw the Londoners forced to wear our yellow away shirts. What a sight for me to behold as a 13 year old: NUFC home vs NUFC away!

This player-worn number 18 (with running repairs) came to me via a former club apprentice.

In pre-season, new match shirts used to be made up by the kit man and numbered 1-22 for two full teams. Shirts from 13 onwards weren't then used by first-teamers, but they did appear in friendly matches, in official full squad team photos and reserve games.

Old photos often show backroom staff wearing high-numbered shirts, which could also be used as spares if a shirt numbered 2-12

16

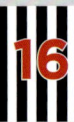

STEVE CARNEY

1981/82 - Division Two

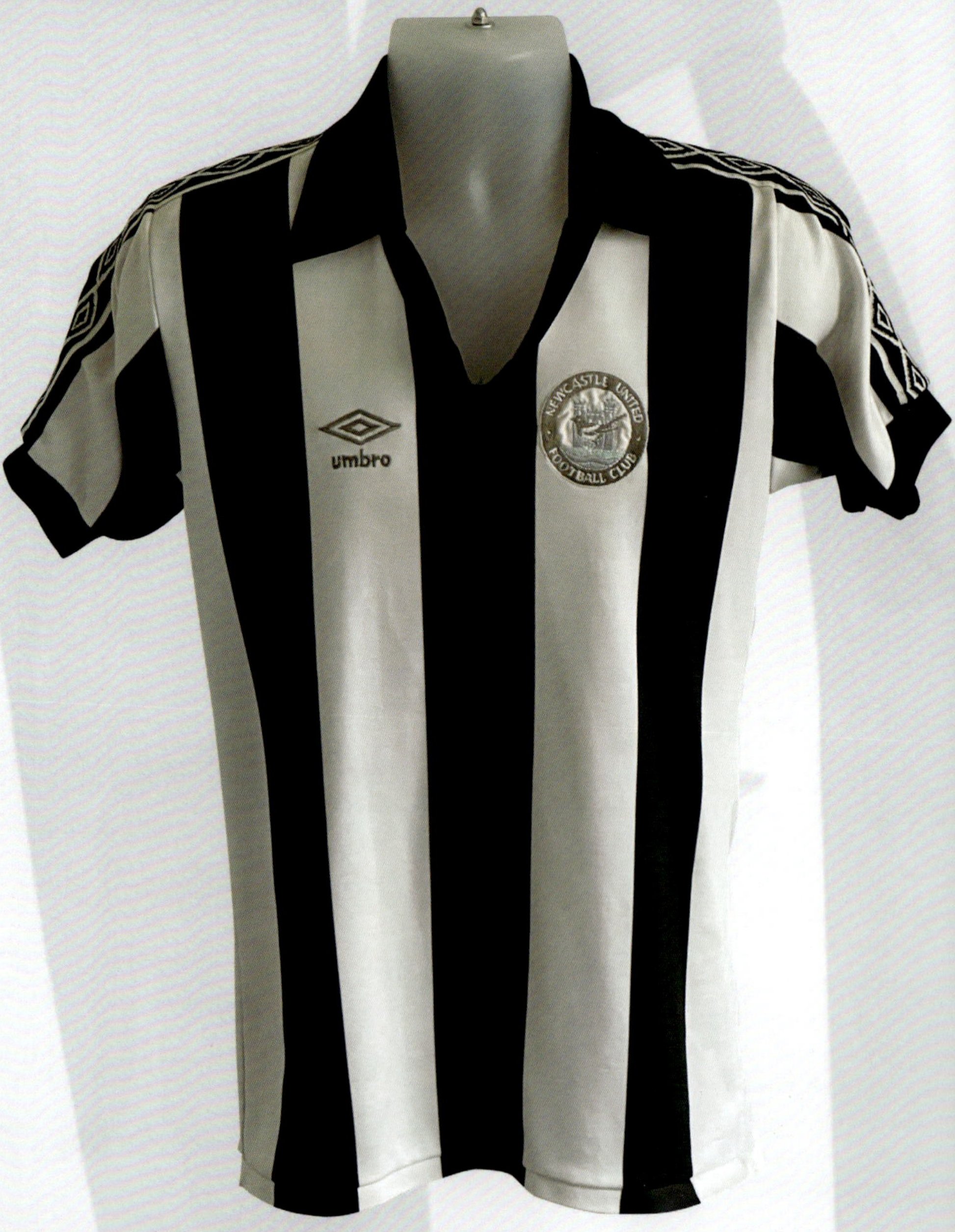

Umbro were founded in Manchester in 1920, and have been making football kits since 1924 when the HUMphreys BROthers, Harold and Wallace, set up a workshop in Wilmslow.

In those less ostentatious days, labels were worn strictly on the inside of clothes, so Umbro's classic kits remained anonymous for a little matter of five decades, during which time the company's client list was a private matter. Quite unthinkable in today's terms.

Umbro started making Newcastle United's kit in 1980, when the home and away shirts became the club's first to feature a manufacturer logo opposite the crest. The shirts remained unchanged in this second season, another unlikely event in the modern era.

Now a public matter, Umbro's iconic diamond logo didn't only appear on the right breast but also in multiple patterns on the logo tape affixed down the shirt sleeves and the sides of the shorts, as well as around the sock tops.

This number six shirt was worn many times by defender Steve Carney in televised matches, where the regular sponsored shirts were not allowed to be worn.

IMRE VARADI
1982/83 - Division Two

There's always been something especially iconic about a Newcastle United number nine shirt. It's recognised right across British football. And this long-sleeved jersey is no exception, given a further lift by the addition of the cloth blue star sponsor and its positive associations.

It was well worn (note the colours washed out of the crest) solely by Imre Varadi throughout '81/82 and '82/83. He was top scorer both seasons with 20 and 22 strikes.

Varadi joined us from Everton in the summer of 1981, and played 90 times with that handsome return of 42 goals before moving on to Sheffield Wednesday in August 1983.

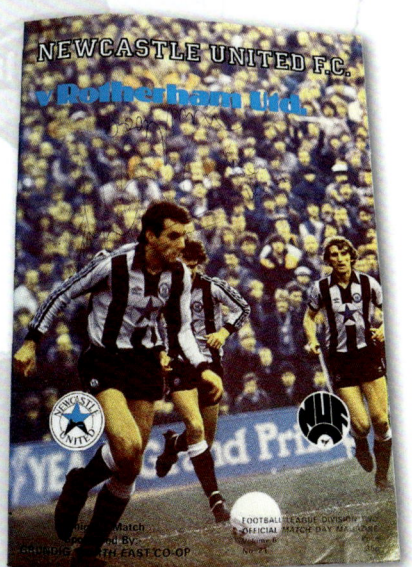

'Ray' is one of my favourite ever NUFC players. He scored a fantastic individual goal against Charlton at St James' Park in November 1981, racing the whole length of the pitch and beating several players; shame it wasn't captured by the TV cameras.

I was one of the 42,000 at Hillsborough in November 1983 when Ray scored two goals for Sheffield Wednesday, as we suffered a 4-2 defeat. His expression said it all after he scored, backed up by a refusal to celebrate.

41

18 IMRE VARADI
1983 - Japan Cup

NEWCASTLE UNITED F.C. FAR EAST TOUR 1983.

Left to Right (Back Row): Ian Liversedge (Physiotherapist), Mick Martin, Neil Macdonald, Peter Haddock, Wes Saunders, Kevin Carr, Jeff Clarke, Martin Thomas, Chris Hedworth, Chris Waddle, Justin Robson, Steve Carney, Ian McFaul (Coach). Front Row: John Anderson, John Trewick, John Trewick, Paul Ferris, David McCreery, Kevin Keegan, Arthur Cox (Manager), Terry McDermott, Chris White, Kenny Wharton, Imre Varadi, John Trewick.

Now this is seriously rare: Imre Varadi's number nine Aertex match shirt from NUFC's Asian tour in the summer of 1983. Along the way we defeated Japan 4-0 and Yamaha (Japan) 1-0, drawing 1-1 with Syria and 0-0 with Botafogo (Brazil) to lift the silverware at the 1983 Kirin Cup (Japan Cup).

John Anderson confirmed that the shirt was prepared for the game against Botafogo, who also wear black and white stripes; but in the end they changed to white, so we never wore this shirt specially made with the intense heat in mind.

The term 'performance fabric' is well-known in sporting circles these days, the accent on comfort, coolness and air flow in the heat of battle. Long gone are the days of scratchy, starchy garments. So it's strange to relate that NUFC were hardly cutting-edge back in 1983. In fact, Aertex was established by Lancashire mill owner Lewis Haslam in 1888!

19 NUMBER 18
1984/85 - Division Two

A Second Division number 18 player-worn shirt which came to me via David McCreery's personal collection.

The shirt itself is a classic in grey with black pinstripes, made from 70 per cent nylon fabric which gives it a shimmering, shiny look. The iconic blue star was the perfect addition, and likewise the black felt number combination to the reverse.

The shirt was worn for two seasons – 1983/84 in the Second Division and 1984/85 back up in in the First.

The round 'NUFC' club crest was only in use for five seasons, but it's a fan favourite. It definitely carries an echo of the famous '70s Leeds United 'smiley' badge.

Great memories of the shirt include seeing KK peeling away after scoring the equaliser at Fulham in front of the TV cameras in March 1984. Also, I was there to witness the promotion to the First Division on May Day at Huddersfield, courtesy of a British Rail Football Special. We only needed a point to go up, and got it in typical Newcastle fashion, coming from 2-0 down to draw 2-2 in front of the travelling Mags packed into three sides of the ground. Going up, Going up!

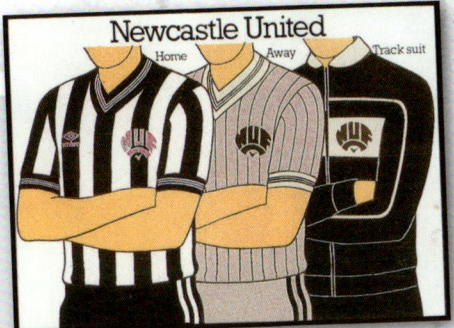

20 PAUL GASCOIGNE
1985/86 - Division One

This shirt is so aesthetically pleasing – simple and classy, and a total change from the home shirts worn earlier in the decade. The blue star was the perfect addition to the coolest of shirts, supplemented by the striped V-neck and cuffs, and of course the red number eight on the back.

This is a matchworn long-sleeved version from 1985/86, mainly worn by the legendary Paul Gascoigne, who first came to prominence this season, playing 35 games and scoring nine goals. The shirt was also worn by David McCreery in the remainder of matches.

Gazza went on to make 104 appearances, scoring 25 goals in his NUFC career, however the destructive instability at the club meant we couldn't prevent the gifted young player from leaving.

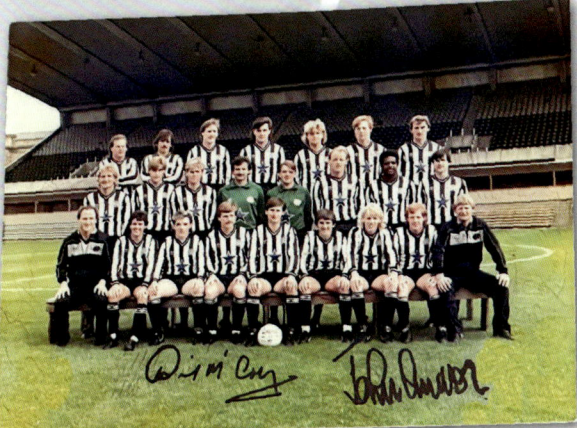

It was one of the saddest days for Magpies fans when Gazza headed off to Spurs at only 21 years of age in the summer of 1988.

47

21 PAUL STEPHENSON
1986/87 - Division One

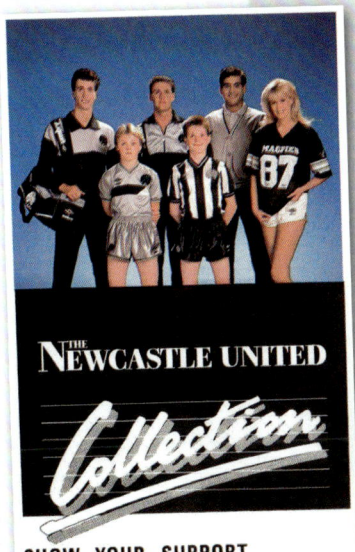

THE NEWCASTLE UNITED Collection

SHOW YOUR SUPPORT
Unique – the team's very own look for sports and leisure. With the distinctive style, quality and prestige of the match kit, training and off the field wear worn by the players themselves. Made by Umbro, the club's official supplier. There are designs and sizes to suit most members of the family. There's no mistaking the real thing – every garment bears the authentic team badge and the distinctive Umbro diamond trade mark.

IT'S ONLY AUTHENTIC IF IT'S UMBRO

1986/87 season. However, back in these days before the introduction of squad numbers and player names to shirts, Alan Davies, Ian Bogie, Neil McDonald, Darren Jackson, Andy Thomas and (on one occasion) Paul Gascoigne also took their turns in the sought-after number seven.

For much of the season it looked as though Willie McFaul's men were destined for relegation to Division Two, however a magical late resurgence in form, with a record-breaking scoring run by Paul Goddard at its heart, eventually secured NUFC's safety.

In the summer of 1986, NUFC shirt sponsorship was taken over by another brewery, this time the Cheshire-based Greenall Whitley & Company.

Initially, the logo featured on the front of the shirts was 'Greenalls Beers', though this was soon updated, mid season – not, as you might have expected, to correct the missing apostrophe, but instead to remove the company's subtle little goddess logo and reduce the text simply to 'Greenalls'.

This long-sleeved shirt was worn in the main by Paul Stephenson during the

49

22 | JOHN ANDERSON
1986/87 - Division One

This short-sleeved number eleven shirt was worn on many occasions during 1986/87 by our versatile Irish international stopper John Anderson.

For me, it stands out as a testament to the benefits of social media as a tool for all of us collectors.

This 'Greenalls'-sponsored variant had been a missing link in my collection for many years, so after my introduction to Twitter in 2014, I put out a 'Please help' post in the hope of finding someone who had the shirt. This went on for three years, without any luck.

Then, in late 2017, thanks to a good friend, Alan 'Old Toon Fan' Golightly, a shirt was located! Alan was able to connect me with its owner, Mark Roberts, who had posted on Twitter having worn it for a non-uniform day at work, and finally agreed to part company with it. What better way to use social media and all those friendly connections than to demonstrate a shared love of our football club.

'Ando' surely represents NUFC's greatest bargain in post-war history, joining on a free from Preston in the summer of 1982. His arrival was low key as the club had recently signed Kevin Keegan; but Ando gave outstanding service for a full decade and was granted a testimonial by the club. He retired in 1992, having made 337 appearances and scored 15 goals.

23 NEIL McDONALD
1987/88 - Division One

A classic shirt design for 1987/88 featured a white wrapover collar, a diamond shadow pattern and a white sublimated bar across the front of the shirt, with the black 'Greenalls' text in felt ('Beers' having been consigned to the slop tray midway through the previous season).

This short-sleeved number seven shirt was mainly worn by Neil McDonald and also by Darren Jackson over the course of the campaign.

The highlights of the season were undoubtedly the signing of the Brazil international Mirandinha and the outstanding form of Paul Gascoigne, which both contributed to an eighth-place finish, our highest since promotion back to the top flight.

Personal memories of this shirt include the trip to Old Trafford in September 1997 which saw an inspired two-goal performance from Mira in a 2-2 draw (plus a whole weekend spent sampling the delights of Stretford). Also, a cracking 2-0 New Year's Day win at much-fancied Nottingham Forest, after a drink-fuelled decision to get the first train to Nottingham that morning. And not forgetting Kenny Wharton sitting on the ball against Luton at St James' Park!

24 PAUL GASCOIGNE
1987/88 - Division One

Worn throughout the 1987/88 season by one of NUFC's most iconic and cherished players, this cool grey away shirt was one of several '80s styles where Umbro employed blocky panels to striking effect.

This design was worn for three seasons, from 1985-88, the first season with the blue star and the remaining two with Greenalls as sponsor.

The shirt itself has been well worn in battle and has the scars to show for it, having been ripped from the neck down to the bottom of the black panel and then repaired unprofessionally with good old-fashioned stitching.

Gazza played 35 times, scoring seven goals in the First Division this season, his last for the club, wearing this shirt every time it was used, and picking up the PFA Young Player of the Year award for his troubles – which were few and far between in this effortlessly brilliant phase of his career.

Personal memories of this shirt include the trip to Hillsborough in August 1987, when the lads won 1-0 courtesy of a fortuitous Darren Jackson goal – and then we all got drenched walking back to the car parked near the train station. Happy days.

25 | NUMBER SIX
1988/89 - Division One

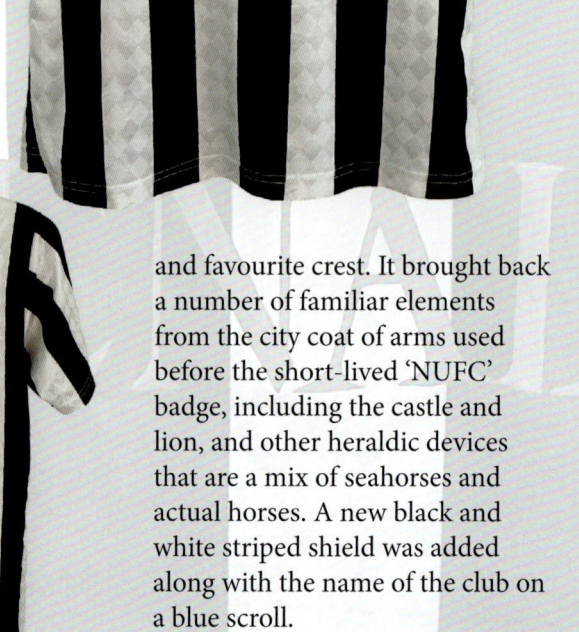

On this matchworn number six shirt from early in the 1988/89 season, note how the sponsor text is green in colour and flush to the surface of the material – and so barely legible from any distance.

That's why there was soon a move to rethink the presentation of the Greenalls sponsor logo as a matter of urgency.

Also new for this season was the club's current, longest-lasting and favourite crest. It brought back a number of familiar elements from the city coat of arms used before the short-lived 'NUFC' badge, including the castle and lion, and other heraldic devices that are a mix of seahorses and actual horses. A new black and white striped shield was added along with the name of the club on a blue scroll.

NUMBER FOUR
1988/89 - Division One

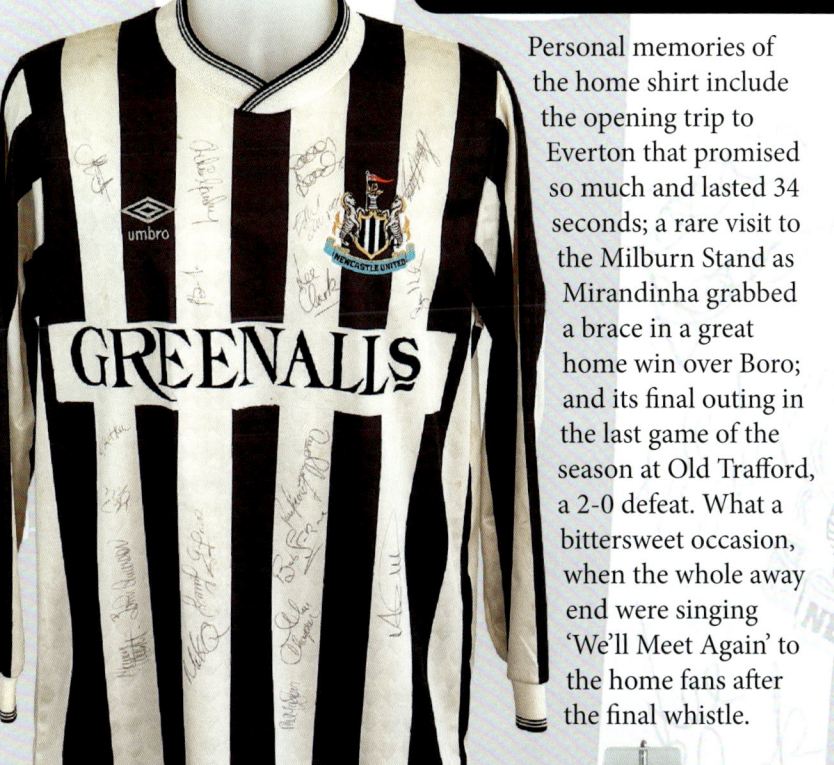

26

Personal memories of the home shirt include the opening trip to Everton that promised so much and lasted 34 seconds; a rare visit to the Milburn Stand as Mirandinha grabbed a brace in a great home win over Boro; and its final outing in the last game of the season at Old Trafford, a 2-0 defeat. What a bittersweet occasion, when the whole away end were singing 'We'll Meet Again' to the home fans after the final whistle.

Fully signed by the squad, this matchworn number four features the sponsor logo in a newly added white bar. It's much more visible; but strangely it was changed yet again later in the season to green writing in the bar! The sponsor logo troubles were symbolic of a dreadful '88/89 season that ended up with relegation to Division Two.

57

27 NUMBER 15
1988/89 - Division One

This green and yellow away shirt was much loved by the fans, my own example being the player-worn First Division squad number 15.

Memories of an Umbro classic include the intoxicated (me, not the team!) 2-0 defeat at Derby County in September 1988, which came after a pre-match bomb scare, and saw Paul Goddard get one against his old club. Then there was the win at Sheffield Wednesday on Boxing Day, an early 10.30 kick-off where I was chuffed to make a fleeting appearance on the official video release of the match.

The 1988/89 away shirt was only worn six times, its other appearances coming in League matches at Luton, Tottenham, Southampton and Sheffield United.

Strangely, Michael O'Neill and Rob MacDonald were the only players ever to score in this Umbro design, both contributing to that 2-1 Boxing Day victory at Hillsborough.

Here we see Mick Quinn wearing the shirt soon after he signed for Newcastle United in the summer of 1989.

59

28 | NUMBER 17
1989/90 - Division Two

60

Uncle Billy had reported that he'd originally been gifted the shirt by Mick Quinn, so the very least I could do is follow up. In 2003, when Mick was doing a local personal appearance at WH Smith for the launch of his book, *Who Ate All the Pies?*, I joined the lengthy queue and asked him to personally sign it for me.

A particular memory of this shirt is wearing it at Wembley for the 2000 FA Cup semi-final against Chelsea, which we sadly lost 2-1.

Much loved and treasured, this was my first ever player-worn shirt. The squad number 17 shirt from the Second Division campaign of 1989/90.

It arrived into my possession in the summer of 1992, having travelled with my wonderful mother all the way from the USA. I have to thank her for all the hard work in securing the shirt from my Uncle Billy. It was during her visit to my auntie and uncle's in Pennsylvania for their silver wedding that she convinced him to part with it and brought it back for me. To say I was overjoyed is an understatement.

29 KEVIN DILLON
1989/90 - Division Two

This long-sleeved number four away shirt was matchworn on ten occasions during the 1989/90 season, mostly by Kevin Dillon but also by Roy Aitken.

Memories of this fine green and yellow style include the trip to Brighton in October 1989 when the supporters' bus we were on broke down at Toddington services, and we didn't get to the Goldstone Ground until the second half – however, a 3-0 win courtesy of a Mick Quinn hat-trick softened the blow.

With a massive share war behind the scenes and fans being urged to boycott the matches, it seemed unlikely that NUFC would bounce straight back after relegation to Division Two. Nevertheless, I ended up attending 55 of the 58 games in all competitions, travelling far and wide to Brighton, Plymouth and Bournemouth.

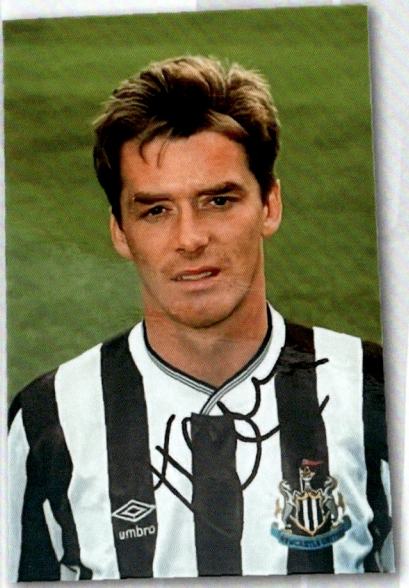

NUFC ended the season in third place, which unfortunately meant the Play-offs. Against Sunderland. Who had finished the season six points behind us in sixth. This shirt was worn in the first-leg scoreless draw away at Roker; but the second leg at St James' Park didn't go well, a catastrophic 2-0 defeat signalling a further stay in the Second Division.

JOHN BURRIDGE
1989/90 - Division Two

and kit manufacturers allowed it before the strictures of shirt sponsorship grew ever tighter.

As Budgie had a glove contract with Uhlsport, they would also have privately agreed to provide shirts for him to wear, giving more exposure to the brand.

Budgie wore this fabulous goalkeeper shirt in a hard-fought 0-0 draw against West Ham at Upton Park on 11th November 1989.

During his time in Newcastle, John was also known to wear Uhlsport goalkeeper shirts in matches, as well as his seasonal sets of different Umbro jerseys. Back then, keepers were free to wear any shirt they wanted,

For the West Ham match, however, he wore this blue striped Umbro number one shirt, additionally tagged with their 'No.1' logo. It features heavily padded shoulders and arms, a stylish shadow-stripe pattern and the Greenalls sponsor in white.

31 **RAY RANSON**
1990 - Norrie McCathie Testimonial

There may be a few fans out there scratching their heads over this shirt. What do you mean, you don't recall the name of Norrie McCathie? The man was a club legend. And the shirt collectors amongst you will certainly recognise that this one-off NUFC shirt prepared for his testimonial match is much sought after and incredibly hard to find.

McCathie played a club record 576 games between 1981 and 1996, and was richly deserving of the testimonial match awarded for ten seasons' service back in 1990 – with Newcastle United the honoured opposition chosen to take on Norrie's own Dunfermline Athletic.

Unusually for the time, this was one match when the players of Newcastle United turned out in official replica shirts rather than their usual player-issue jerseys. The shirt is identifiable as such because of the embossed crest and Umbro badge; but it does also feature custom-embroidered match detailing in an off-centre circular pattern.

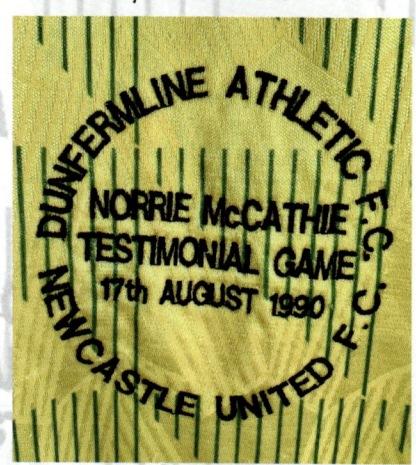

This number two shirt was worn in the pre-season scoreless draw by right-back Ray Ranson.

32 | MARK McGHEE
1990/91 - Division Two

The long-sleeved number ten shirt that was matchworn by Mark McGhee on several occasions between August and December 1990.

When the famous/infamous 'Barcode' style first came out, it was considered a very radical move in the utilisation of the black and white stripes.

The Umbro design incorporated a half-and-half mix of thin and thick stripes on the front body of the shirt, and thick stripes on the back. Meanwhile, one one arm was thin stripes and the other thick stripes.

True, a description of the shirt sounds like a recipe for disaster; but with the benefit of hindsight it's generally viewed as a design classic. The 'Greenalls' sponsor logo was sublimated in black in the shirt design, which also saw Football League arm badges worn for the first time.

Scottish striker Mark McGhee's second spell with the club (1989-91, 67 League games, 24 goals) proved more successful than the first (1977-79, 28 and 5), shortly before he went on to make a name for himself as a manager.

33 | NUMBER NINE
1990/91 - Central League

A matchworn, unsponsored reserve-team home shirt with an embossed crest and Umbro badge, and a stitched number nine on the reverse.

The shirt is very rare, especially with it being an unsponsored version.

The shirt was specially gifted to me by the club after the Oldham Athletic home game which we won 3-2 on 13th April 1991.

The match was one of the most exciting of the season, Newcastle cruising to 3-0 up with goals from Gavin Peacock, Andy Hunt and Kevin Brock before late goals from Rick Holden and Ian Marshall made it a tense final few minutes for the vast majority of the 16,615 supporters.

At the end of the season the shirt was signed by the whole squad, courtesy of Billy Askew. Notable signatures on the shirt include a 16-year-old Steve Watson who had only broken into the first time a few months earlier, and Pavel Srnicek, who had only recently joined the club from Banik Ostrava in his native Czech Republic. Scott Sloan and John Gallacher both arrived at the club with masses of promise from the Scottish Leagues, though unfortunately both NUFC careers took off and ended very much in a whimper.

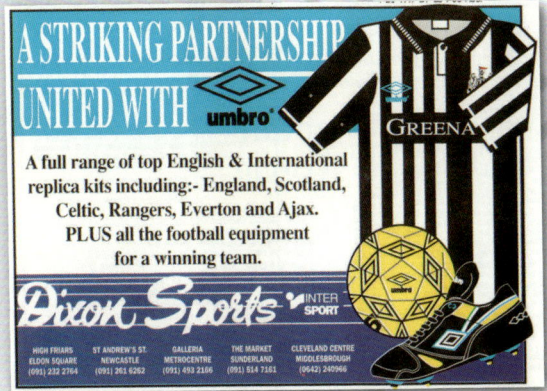

MARK STIMSON
1990/91 - Division Two

In December 1990 Newcastle United had a popular change of sponsors, welcoming back the famous blue star. However, the large plastic affair stuck on the front of the shirt was not the most successful look or marketing tool.

This number three shirt was worn extensively by Mark Stimson during the early part of 1991.

Who can forget the 1991 New Year's Day match at Oldham, and their dreaded plastic pitch? I ventured down on the supporters' bus and witnessed what seemed like a valuable win courtesy of a Mick Quinn left-foot finish midway through the second half – only be denied deep into stoppage time due to Stimson's unfortunate own goal. That result left us in 15th place.

Other memories of this shirt include the away trip to Millwall later that month, a 1-0 win thanks to Gavin Peacock, and two dreadful home matches with Oxford, the first abandoned at half-time. A disappointing campaign, to say the least, finishing eleventh on 59 points. Well and truly a hangover from 1989/90.

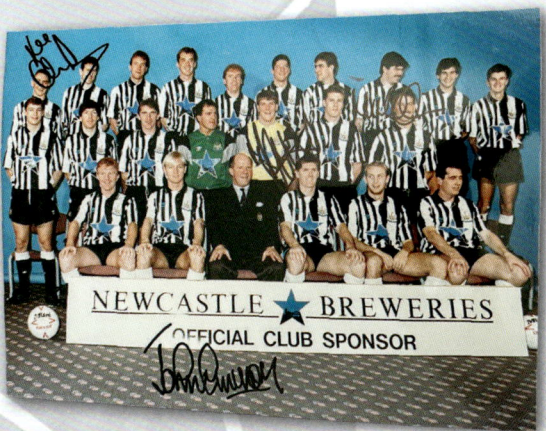

73

35 | MICK QUINN / DAVID KELLY
1991-93 - Division Two

With the blue star back on the home shirt, Newcastle Breweries' parent company Scottish & Newcastle opted to promote the more widely sold McEwan's Lager on the change shirt, which was worn between January 1991 and May 1993.

This iconic number nine was worn with distinction by Mick Quinn and David Kelly throughout this time. They've both since kindly autographed the shirt at separate talk-ins, Mick (who signed 'No 9') speaking passionately about his love of NUFC and great moments over his 140 appearances in which he scored 71 goals. What a character. Ned signed the shirt 'Goalscorer', to which I commented, "You were more than just a goalscorer, mate!"

Personal memories of the shirt include an unforgettable display at Notts County in April 1991, and the momentous evening at Grimsby in May 1993 when NUFC won the First Division title and sealed promotion to the Promised Land of the Premiership.

36 DAVID KELLY
1992/93 - Division Two

The 1992/93 season was all systems go, with everyone's focus firmly fixed on the aim of the newly formed Premiership. The lads kicked off in unbelievable style, recording no less than eleven straight consecutive victories at the start of the season.

And, by the end of the campaign, we had successfully stormed into the big league, finishing eight points clear of second-placed West Ham by winning 29 games and scoring 92 goals.

This is David Kelly's number nine shirt from his own personal collection, which was worn in the penultimate game of this remarkable season – the last match we ever turned out in Umbro, against Oxford on 6th May 1993.

Over the course of the season Ned made 57 League and cup appearances, and finished as top goalscorer with 28.

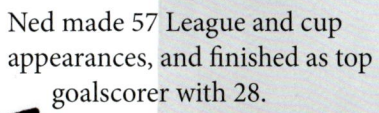

Features of the shirt include the square-styled, Umbro-branded numeral on the reverse, embroidered crest and Umbro badges, sublimated blue star and Football League badges on each arm. It still has white marks on the number from the pitch lines.

37 KEVIN SCOTT
1992/93 - Division Two

A rare matchworn number five McEwan's Lager long-sleeved shirt, pulled on for the televised Division Two fixture against Sunderland on 25th April 1993.

Kevin Scott played 45 League matches in this great promotion season, and wore the number five throughout.

However, despite some top performances on the park, quality control off the field was rather poor when the shirt was made. Instead of the intended home Umbro style of one sleeve with thick stripes and the other with thin, this shirt has both arms with the same thick stripes. Video footage from the era clearly shows several players sporting shirts with a jumbled mix of styles.

MARK ROBINSON
1992/93 - Division Two

38

intended contrast of one thick and one thin. But hey, at least the lads won the match 1-0 with a Scott Sellars goal!

Mark often found himself wearing the number 14, appearing mostly as a sub after joining from Barnsley in March 1993.

Again, the shirt is fully signed by the 1993/94 squad, probably for the purpose of gifting or auctioning off via local charities at the end of the season.

Following on from the shirt opposite, here's another example from that fated TV game against Sunderland in 1993. Here we see the number 14 shirt, benchworn by Mark Robinson, had the exact opposite problem of its number five counterpart. This time, both of the shirt sleeves feature thin stripes instead of the

79

39

DAVID KELLY
1992/93 - Division Two

One of my favourite ever NUFC shirts, this being David Kelly's actual matchworn hat-trick shirt from the brilliant team performance that destroyed Leicester 7-1 on the final day of the 1992/93 campaign. This was the catalyst for the rollercoaster ride of Keegan's 'Entertainers' over the next few years.

Kelly scored a first-half hat-trick in his last game for the club, with a bullet header on 28 minutes, a left-foot shot on 34 and another class header on 45. Andy Cole also notched a hat-trick, with Rob Lee also hitting the net.

NUFC premiered the new ASICS shirt for this game, complete with Football League badges on the arms, embroidered crest and cloth manufacturer badge.

The shirt came from David's own personal collection in 2017. Soon after, he invited me down to a Port Vale home match where he was coaching at the time. We discussed the shirt itself and its meaning, and he duly signed the number for me.

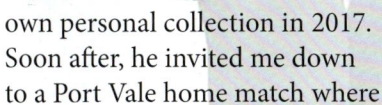

What a shirt, what a game, what a player. In just 18 months at the club he played 83 games and scored 39 goals, including perhaps NUFC's most precious goal, preventing relegation to Division Three in our darkest ever era.

40 MALCOLM ALLEN
1993/94 - Premier League

After promotion to the FA Carling Premiership, this shirt was matchworn against Everton on 25th August 1993, when we won 1-0 in front of 34,833 at St James' Park. Malcolm scored the only goal in NUFC's first ever Premier League win.

The shirt was made by ASICS, which opened for business as the Onitsuka Co in 1949, when Kihachiro Onitsuka began manufacturing basketball shoes in his home town of Kobe, Japan. The name is an acronym for the Latin proverb, *anima sana in corpore sano* – 'pray for a sound mind in a sound body'.

This was the manufacturer's sole home offering, plain but as classy as you could get, the black and white stripes adorned only with black cuffs and touches of blue trimming, particularly effective on the two-button collar.

In 1993 ASICS was in the midst of a big expansion into English football, though today they are no longer active in this country.

On this specific shirt the number was a square style, unbranded on a black patch stitched on to the back of the shirt. Blue star shirts were worn in non-televised matches.

KEVIN SCOTT
41 — 1993/94 - Premier League

After promotion to the FA Premier League, the new black and white home shirt featured the McEwan's Lager sponsor for televised matches. For the first three home games (against Spurs, Coventry and Manchester United), the logo appeared in yellow lettering, which unfortunately proved barely legible.

Thereafter, a black patch appeared on the shirts with white lettering. What wasn't widely known was that the panel was fastened over the yellow writing, as evidenced when Steve Howey's shirt was damaged against Blackburn, exposing the quick alteration work.

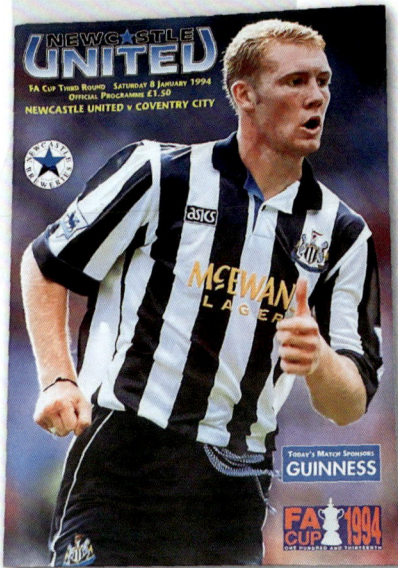

For years this shirt had eluded me; however, after a friend pointed out the story, I checked the inside of this shirt and could plainly see signs of a raised yellow sponsor which was hidden away underneath the black patch.

As I had another shirt from the same season with exactly the same sponsor modification, I then removed as much as I could of the patch on this shirt, fully exposing the original yellow logo – so now it is here to stay.

42 ROB LEE
1993/94 - Premier League

The matchworn shirt that accompanied Newcastle and England midfielder Rob Lee throughout the 1993/94 season, and which can boast the impeccable provenance of coming from the player's own personal collection.

The shirt contains the first version of the black McEwan's Lager patch which was fixed over the original yellow embossed sponsors writing.

Described as 'a blue-chip player' by Sir Bobby Robson, Rob made 381 appearances and scored 56 goals during his ten seasons at the club, which earned him a testimonial match in 2001.

Personal memories for me include the time Rob scored a bullet header in the FA Cup semi-final against Chelsea at Wembley Stadium in April 2000. Then I was among the excitable crowd of Mags at Antwerp in September 1994 when he became the first Newcastle player to score a hat-trick in Europe.

And, finally, there's no forgetting that match against Brentford at St James' Park in March 1993, when Lee scored a goal from inside his own half – though, sorry to say, it was disallowed!

43 — ANDY COLE
1993-95 - Premier League

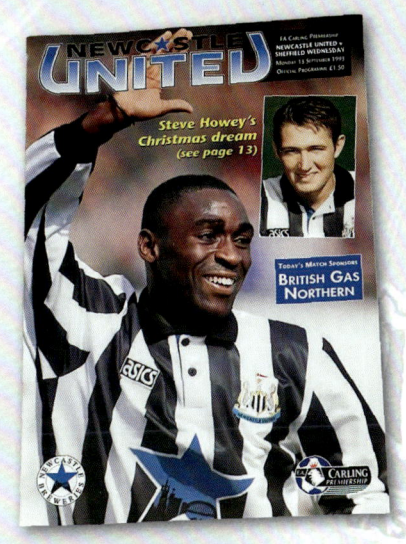

A shirt that brings images and emotions flooding back from King Cole's memorable season.

Like Andy himself, the shirt is a big fan's favourite, this being the long-sleeved version that was strangely never available as a replica even though it was worn for two seasons.

The blue away shirt was used nine times over 1993/94 and 1994/95, featuring a brushstroke effect and supplemented by the McEwan's Lager sponsor in white. This was the decision of Newcastle Breweries' parent company Scottish & Newcastle, who wanted to use the change shirt to promote the popular lager rather than Brown Ale.

The first time it appeared was entirely by accident, at St James' Park, for the televised game against Sheffield Wednesday in September 1993. This after the Owls arrived with a kit that clearly clashed with Newcastle's home strip, forcing us to wear the new blue away strip.

This shirt was worn by Andy during his record-breaking 1993/94 season in which he scored 41 goals. Overall he made 84 appearances, scoring 68 goals in only 22 months at the club. A real cult figure, he was. Who could ever forget the chant...

"Andy Cole, Andy Cole, Andy, Andy Cole. He gets the ball and scores a goal, Andy, Andy Cole..."

PETER BEARDSLEY
1993/94 - Premier League

The first ever 'third shirt' in Newcastle United's history was only ever worn in one game in each of the two seasons under ASICS – both at Sheffield Wednesday. This shirt was worn in the first game, a 1-0 win at Hillsborough on 5th March 1994.

The shirt itself was an ASICS template used by a total of seven clubs between 1993 to 1996, our version being a green shirt with thin, dark-blue chalk stripes.

Absolute quality was Pedro in both spells as player, signing in September 1983 and departing for a record transfer fee in July 1987, having made 164 appearances and scoring 61 goals. He then returned in July 1993 after we'd won promotion to the Premier League as Division One champions, going on to make a further 162 appearances, scoring 58 goals before his final departure as a player in August 1997.

I met him many years later at the training ground where he signed the shirt. In my opinion Peter is the greatest ever NUFC player, his fantastic record across both spells proving what a wonderful and special footballer he was.

45

ANDY COLE
1994/95 - Premier League

This matchworn shirt from the 1994/95 season is fully signed by the squad, featuring a newly reduced-size McEwan's Lager patch, an embroidered crest and embossed ASICS logo.

Over the seasons 1993/94 and 1994/95, NUFC played 104 competitive matches. The brilliant MuseumOfJerseys.com website tells us black and white stripes were worn in 93 of them, the McEwan's logo appearing 59 times versus the blue star's 34.

Compare the variation of badge and logo placement on the shirts below: the ASICS jerseys were produced featuring two alternate positions, for which there's no rational explanation apart from the possibility that they were produced by different suppliers. Or could it just have been production flaws in the manufacturer's finishing process that was responsible for these huge discrepancies?

46 JOHN BERESFORD
1994/95 - UEFA Cup

The shirt worn by Bez against Athletic Bilbao in the UEFA Cup second round, second leg match in the old San Mamés Stadium, 1st November 1994.

This was a memorable campaign for Newcastle supporters. Our first official European venture since 1977. Sadly, the UEFA Cup story of late 1994 was a short one, though there was still plenty of time for the usual rollercoaster narrative and all its attendant emotions. Here we go again.

Swashbuckling as ever, we started out in mid September with a 5-0 win in Antwerp, following up 5-2 in the return…

The lads then roared into a 3-0 lead at home to Athletic Bilbao… before two late goals – and then a solitary goal by the Basques in Spain – meant that by the start of November we were out of the competition on the away-goal rule.

The shirt was swapped with Athletic's Aitor Larrazábal, and came from his personal collection. The embossed ASICS logo on this shirt was different to the normal design as it showed the manufacturer's logo as well as the company name. The shirt also has a plain stitched number three on a patch on the reverse.

47

PAVEL SRNICEK
1994/95 - Premier League

Nothing says 1990s football more than a Technicolor ASICS goalkeeper shirt.

The 'broken glass' template shirt was worn on a number of occasions by Pavel Srnicek during the 1994/95 season.

When Pav returned in 2006 for an unexpected, short second spell, he was named as sub for the home match against Manchester United, and was warming up by the sidelines next to the Milburn paddock where I sat before the game.

At that time, there was only a limited chance of him actually playing or being part of the matchday squad, so I'd decided to take the shirt along to the match in the hope of seeing him.

Now this opportunity allowed me to beckon the reserve goalie over and show him the shirt. He came over immediately, and was visibly made up by what I had brought along and managed to show him. We reminisced about those successful times, and he then kindly signed the shirt for me.

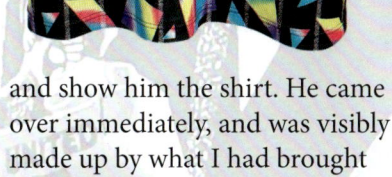

Always much loved and sorely missed.

"Pavel is a Geordie."

48 **LES FERDINAND**
1995/96 - Premier League

The first Adidas shirt worn by Newcastle United, and the choice of many fans as one of the club's greatest ever. This fine example was matchworn against Aston Villa on 14th April 1996, when Les Ferdinand himself scored the winner in a 1-0 victory.

Newcastle gave Adidas the freedom to be creative and to design kits that were consistent with the vision of Sir John Hall, Freddy Shepherd and the club's executives to make the Magpies a major force on and off the field.

The manufacturer's head of football business wrote the original strategy for the eight-year partnership with the help of Newcastle's board, protesting his belief that "the way you look in your work is massively important to the way you perform."

The club wanted to make a statement because they had ambition. They came very close to winning the Premier League, so the kits were really well-timed in terms of the buzz and the hype and investment that was being ploughed into the club at the time.

Is this the greatest shirt that has ever graced the Premier League? I believe it is. Looking back at it now, the quality, the purity and timeless style of the shirt make it one of the greatest I have ever seen.

49 PHILIPPE ALBERT
1996 - Stuart Pearce Testimonial

At the same venue that effectively blew our title chances, United soon returned to the City Ground to provide the opposition in the Stuart Pearce Testimonial on 8th May 1996.

Our long-standing commitment to appear in this game had been mocked days previously by the Manchester United boss Alex Ferguson – who questioned whether Forest would go easy on Newcastle in that preceding League game.

That then resulted in Kevin Keegan giving his infamous "love it..." speech to Sky cameras following Newcastle's televised 1-0 victory at Leeds – his emotional response to Fergie mentioning Pearce by name, a reference that passed many viewers by at the time.

Coming five days after the final competitive game of the season, this enjoyable evening was a decent way to help make up for our disappointment. A near full-strength side was augmented late on by Keegan and assistant McDermott. The former netted from the penalty spot in front of the Toon following, and threw his shirt (complete with rare Adidas logos on the numbers) into the crowd at full time. Likewise Philippe Albert!

50 RUEL FOX
1995/96 - Premier League

Now here's a shirt that many supporters consider an all-time favourite, despite its surprisingly short time in use. This Ruel Fox matchworn example played a part at The Dell on 9th September 1995, when the lads went down 1-0 to Southampton.

The iconic first Adidas away shirt was an instant hit. Worn with ecru shorts and maroon socks in late 1995, it represented a stylistic and historical nod to the kit worn by NUFC forerunner club Newcastle West End, who had played at St James' Park over 100 years before.

It was only actually worn in five competitive matches: Bolton 3-1, Sheffield Wednesday 2-0, Southampton 0-1, Stoke City 4-0 and Tottenham 1-1 – the last of which was on 29th October 1995.

Memories of this shirt point me to the Tottenham game which was televised by Sky, David Ginola mesmerising the cameras with his stylish looks, and scoring the equaliser wearing this stunning ensemble.

Ruel Fox also played a wing role in Kevin Keegan's team of 'Entertainers', scoring ten League goals in the 1994/95 season – though ironically it was the arrival of Ginola in June 1995 that led to his slipping down the order.

103

51 PETER BEARDSLEY
1996 - Charity Shield

What an awful match this shirt was issued for: the miserable 4-0 humiliation against Manchester United in the Charity Shield at Wembley on 11th August 1996. As if that weren't bad enough, the heavens opened up afterwards and soaked everybody to the skin. It's a great shirt, though but.

First, take a look at the unique design of the embroidered patch that contained match details. Furthermore, the shirt has a long hem containing three buttons up to the neckline – and it's worth mentioning that, along with the collar, it was white! All of Newcastle's shirts since the late 1960s had featured a collar that was either completely black or had some form of black trim; but this colourless look set the tone for understated style that permeated the rest of the garment.

The black and white stripes were of a perfect width, in my view – wide enough to frame not only the Newcastle badge but also the manufacturer's logo in name form only, set on its own black strip. As a final flourish, Adidas's iconic three stripes also made an appearance; but in reverence to the club and its history, only on the sleeves, not extending on to the shoulders and neck.

52 LEE CLARK
1996/97 - UEFA Cup

Alcohol-related sponsorship was banned in France when Newcastle played Metz in the UEFA Cup third round, first leg on 19th November 1996 – which resulted in this blank shirt with no sponsor.

The club dealt with the problem in the most direct manner, simply by removing the frontal panels and donning sponsorless shirts.

Adding to the unusually plain look of the shirt, the numbers on the back were not augmented by players' names. This shirt was benchworn by Lee Clark, who looked on powerless to influence the 1-1 draw.

A Geordie through and through, Lee came though the NUFC youth system and made his debut in September 1990, quickly becoming a supporters' hero in the '90s, donning the number ten shirt in the PL before passing it to Les Ferdinand and wearing the number 20 in his last season. After reluctantly moving on in June 1997, Lee made an emotional return in 2005 for his final playing season. Overall, he made 265 appearances, scoring 28 goals. He bleeds black and white, his love for the club paramount.

53 DARREN PEACOCK
1996/97 - UEFA Cup

From Darren Peacock's own collection, the number five shirt that he wore in the UEFA Cup quarter-final against Monaco is a real rarity.

Played on 18th March 1997 in the Stade Louis II, the lads sadly lost the second-leg match 3-0. It may have been a famous awayday for the Toon fans who made the trip, but the failure to peg back Monaco's 1-0 lead from the home leg meant the end of another European adventure.

Again, the discrepancy in advertising standards between the UK and France meant we were not allowed to sport the regular Newcastle Brown Ale sponsorship on shirts. In France, alcohol adverts were banned in the same way that tobacco products were outlawed in the UK. But this time the club went one better than just removing the offending sponsor panel. At the time, Scottish & Newcastle Breweries owned the Center Parcs holiday complexes, so a temporary sponsor was installed.

Also of note were the nameless backs. The patch on the bottom front of the shirt was different from the previous season, even though it's the same home shirt.

54 ROBBIE ELLIOTT
1996/97 - Premier League

Plus a sixth if you include Pav.

In the summer of 1997, NUFC's official magazine, *Black and White*, ran a competition to win Robbie's match shirt. All you had to do was answer three questions about Elliott on the postcard provided...

And to my amazement, a month later, I was notified as being the winner. Get in!

Robbie had two good spells at NUFC, 1991-97 and 2001-06, his 188 club appearances interrupted by a successful spell with Bolton.

Newcastle United 5-0 Nottingham Forest. This comprehensive thrashing, served up on 11th May 1997, meant we finished the season as runners-up. Geordies in the Champions League! Well, the qualifying rounds, to be precise...

And this is the very shirt worn by Robbie Elliott when he added the final goal to the four already netted before half-time, scoring with a drive as sweet as any he had ever hit. Robbie was one of five Geordies in the side that day, along with teammates Watson, Clark, Beardsley and Shearer.

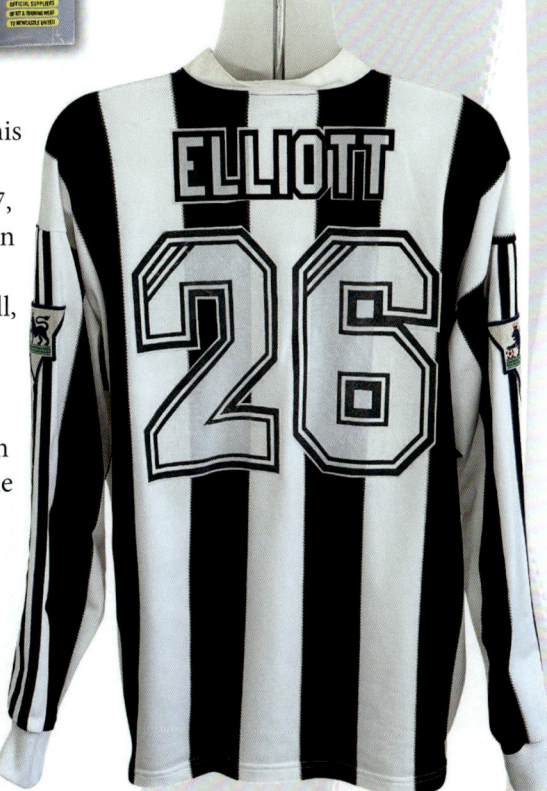

55

DAVID BATTY
1996/97 - UEFA Cup

Ultra-rare, match-prepared number four away shirt which was to be worn by midfield enforcer David Batty against Monaco in the UEFA Cup quarter-final second leg on 18th March 1997.

Research has shown that this shirt was made ready in case of a possible shirt clash; however, as it panned out, Monaco wore their red and white home shirts and NUFC wore our usual home shirt, just as they had both done in the first leg.

This shirt, dubbed 'the denim kit', featured three white hoops on a thick black band across the centre of the shirt, and three white stripes on a thick black V-neck collar.

Normally, this shirt would have been emblazoned with the large Newcastle Brown Ale badge in white; but as the match was played in France, the Center Parcs sponsor was affixed in its place. The embroidered white Adidas logo, in text only, is another cool feature of the shirt.

Specially prepared for this game only, with the rare NUFC numbers only worn in Europe, I have never seen another example of this shirt outside my collection.

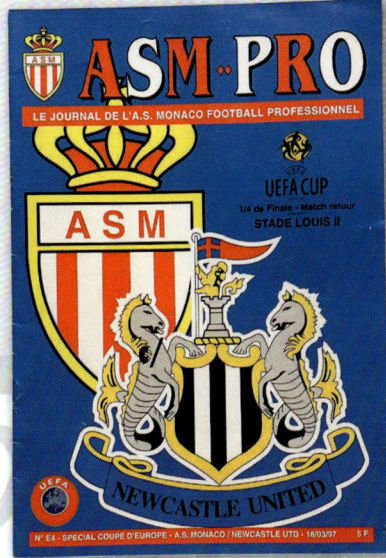

113

56 FAUSTINO ASPRILLA
1997/98 - Champions League

Following the glorious end to the season and the second-place finish, NUFC qualified for the Champions League for the first time after beating Croatia Zagreb in the second qualifying round. The luck of the draw then put us in Group C, facing Barcelona, PSV Eindhoven and Dynamo Kiev.

We began with one of those nights that you dream of, beating the mighty Barcelona 3-2, with Faustino Asprilla – whose match-issued shirt from the campaign features here – scoring a fantastic hat-trick. A 2-2 draw in Kiev was then followed by two uninspiring defeats, as we went down 1-0 and 2-0 to PSV. A trip to Barcelona in late November ended in a 1-0 defeat, and finally there was a 2-0 win over Dynamo Kiev at St James' Park. Unfortunately, NUFC finished third in the group, and the dream was over.

Personal memories for me include celebrating in Walkers nightclub after the Barca victory, and the trip to the Nou Camp for the away match where the home fans boycotted the game. A huge contingent of Mags were stuck up in the gods and all got soaked to the skin. But we still had a cracking time!

115

57 ROB LEE
1998 - FA Cup Final

116

Rob Lee's shirt from the FA Cup final against Arsenal at the old Wembley Stadium on 16th May 1998. NUFC were making their first Cup final appearance in 24 years – a fantastic occasion for a whole new generation of fans among the 79,183 present, despite the disappointment of going down 2-0 on the day.

One-nil down at half-time, Kenny Dalglish's boys fought back in the second half. A Nikos Dabizas header hit the bar, and Alan Shearer hit the inside of David Seaman's post; but the League champions extended their lead shortly afterwards when Nicolas Anelka broke away.

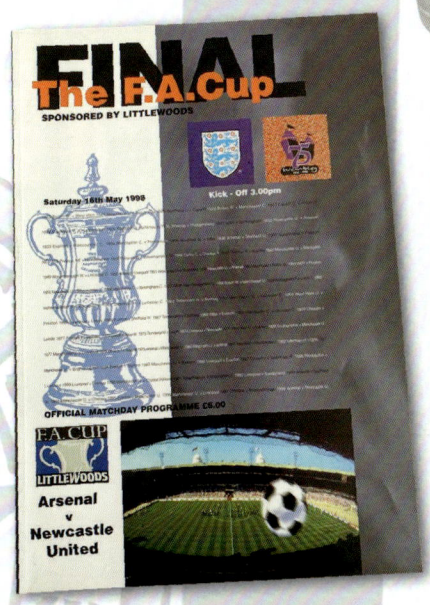

Afterwards, you might have thought Newcastle had won the Cup, given the noise we made – as sporting as ever as Arsenal collected the trophy, and a great drink-fuelled night out in the West End to follow.

It's impossible to say whether this is Rob's shirt that was matchworn for 90 minutes, or his identical spare. It features the special FA Cup final embroidery and Lextra Littlewoods FA Cup sleeve patches.

WARREN BARTON
1998/99 - Cup Winners' Cup

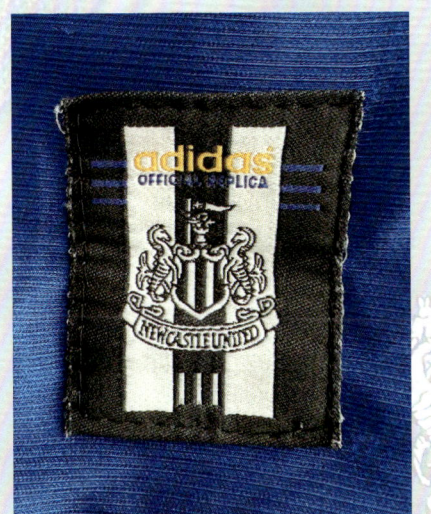

The 1998/99 away kit was premiered in the pre-season JD Sports Cup against Benfica and Boro, and in the prestigious friendly with Juventus. Other outings included Tranmere Rovers away in the League Cup and Partizan in the ECWC, when this shirt was benchworn by Warren Barton in the second leg in Belgrade. The Serbians won 1-0 on the night, edging the tie 2-2 on away goals.

The style was only worn twice in the Premiership, at Derby County and Sheffield Wednesday.

These shirts were absolutely massive, and incredibly shiny. The contrast gold trim and number contributed to a classy blue kit. Quite Interestingly, not all of the players' shirts featured the 'replica' patch.

NUFC.com reminds us how the kit's defining moment came away in Belgrade, with "David Batty's ill-advised tug on the shirt of Vladimir Ivic" right in front of the referee. And "Vuk Rasovic obliged from the spot, just as he had done at Gallowgate two weeks before."

59 JOHN BARNES
1999 - Peter Beardsley Testimonial

Peter Beardsley hadn't completed the ten years of continuous service at SJP required for a 'testimonial' match – so this is John Barnes' matchworn shirt from the 'benefit' match on 27th January 1999.

Celtic dominated the game, going 3-0 up through a Peacock own-goal, Moravcik and Burchill, before Peter Beardsley was given a token gesture of a penalty in the final few seconds. "David Hannah brought down Shearer in the box," the *Glasgow Herald* reported. "The kick was awarded and Beardsley blazed it over the bar, only for the referee to order a retake, from which he finally scored."

The 22 players that represented NUFC and PB's dream team that night were an unreal mix of past and present talent – Hislop, Cole, Howey, Darren Peacock, Pearce, Barton, Barnes, Elliott, Sellars, Kenny and Paul Dalglish, Srnicek, Watson, Shearer, Beresford, Albert Craig, Irvine, Neilson, Gascoigne, Waddle and Keegan. A fitting tribute for a gifted player.

It was such a good night, no one noticed when NUFC finished the game with 14 players on the field!

60 GEORGE GEORGIADIS
1999 - FA Cup Final

Match-issued player's shirt for the FA Cup final against Manchester United at the old Wembley Stadium on 22nd May 1999, in front of 79,301.

This was NUFC's second consecutive appearance in the final, and the first ever that would not be replayed in the event of a draw, instead being decided on the day. Goals from Teddy Sheringham and Paul Scholes gave United a comfortable 2–0 win in a poor game from a NUFC perspective – although, again, the build-up outside The Globe in Baker Street and the night out afterwards in Covent Garden still made the occasion a memorable one. Imagine if we'd won!

NUFC actually premiered the 1999/2000 shirt in this game, with Ruud Gullit requesting white socks with black trim rather than the usual black socks with white trim, citing the success of former teams who had also worn white socks.

All squad players were issued with Cup final shirts, though sadly our Greek international winger didn't make the match-day squad.

61 WARREN BARTON
1999/2000 - UEFA Cup

Back in 1999, when Newcastle United played AS Roma over two legs in the UEFA Cup third round, certain match facts are historically verifiable. Unfortunately, they don't include which of the two games saw Warren Barton swap shirts with Vincent Montella.

What we do know about this European tie is that the away leg at the Stadio Olimpico took place on 25th November 1999. Roma won 1-0 through a Francesco Totti penalty. On 9th December, the return match at St James' Park ended 0-0.

While the Italian international striker played in both games, Barton played the full game in Italy but remained on the bench for the home leg. An exchange clearly took place at some point, as the source of this shirt – with a smaller Brown Ale sponsor logo, minus PL number logos – was Montella's own private collection!

Warren was a great servant, signing from Wimbledon for £4 million in June 1995 and making 220 appearances (scoring five goals) in his seven years at the club. Still fondly remembered on Tyneside, Barton remains a strong advocate of NUFC to this day.

62 | DANIEL CORDONE
2000/01 - Premier League

A bit of a character was Lobo. He had to undergo surgery to remove his soldered earrings after his debut, as players were not allowed to wear jewellery, even when covered up.

Here is his matchworn home shirt from that millennium season, ostensibly the same design as the 1999/00 shirt apart from the new NTL shirt sponsor, and the rather curious addition of the 'official replica' patch on the bottom-right front of the shirt.

Argentine striker Daniel 'Lobo' Cordone began the 2000/01 season in impressive fashion, scoring in the first game at the newly reconstructed St James' Park and going on to make 27 appearances, adding two more goals in his single season on Tyneside.

63 | **CHRISTIAN BASSEDAS**
2001/02 - Rob Lee Testimonial

Argentine international midfielder Christian Bassedas wore this one-off commemorative shirt in Rob Lee's well-deserved testimonial match at St James' Park on 11th August 2001.

Christian played the full game against Athletic Bilbao, which we ended up losing 1-0 in front of a very respectable and appreciative 18,189 crowd.

Bassedas joined Newcastle United in 2000 from Vélez Sarsfield, and in three seasons with the club had a pretty unsuccessful time on Tyneside, making only 33 first-team appearances and scoring just a single goal.

With a brief loan period at CD Tenerife sandwiched in between his NUFC games, he returned to Argentina in 2003 and retired shortly afterwards at the age of 30.

Personal memories for me, I was there at Stamford Bridge in January 2001 when the defensive midfielder scored his first and last goal for Newcastle.

The shirt itself is a cracker, an already-successful shirt for NUFC further enhanced by the wonderful testimonial embroidery and classy typeface.

64 WAYNE QUINN
2001/02 - Intertoto Cup

130

Wayne Quinn's number ten shirt, matchworn against Troyes in the Intertoto Cup final, second leg at St James' Park on 21st August 2001. It's a slight oddity as NUFC wore shirts numbered one to eleven on this occasion, as opposed to squad numbers and names.

After an unexpected opportunity to debut in the Intertoto Cup, our season began on 14th July in the third round, winning 4-0 away and then 1-0 against Lokeren. Then it was 3-2 and 3-1 against 1869 Munich in the semi-final. In the final we met Troyes, drawing 0-0 in France before the memorable second leg at SJP which ended in a 4-4 draw – this after taking the lead, going 4-1 down and pulling it back to level, only to lose on away goals.

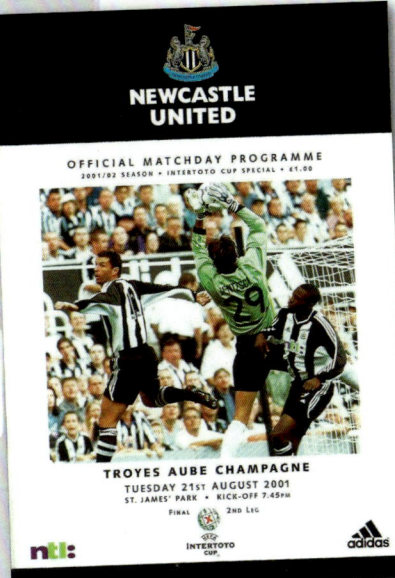

Unbelievably, over 100,000 fans attended the three Intertoto home games. Wayne Quinn scored the first goal of the campaign, his only strike in a total of 24 games.

The Intertoto proved a useful catalyst for a highly successful season where we finished fourth in the PL, making the 2002/03 Champions League qualifiers.

65 SHAY GIVEN
2001/02 - Premier League

Shay Given's goalkeeper shirt worn away at Derby County on 13th April 2002. The shirt came into my possession via the family of the Rams' goalkeeping coach a couple of years later.

This was a typical roller-coaster of an away game – from 2-0 down to turning it around to win 3-2. Memories include Robert and Dyer scoring in quick succession, then Lua Lua scoring the winner in the last minute amidst amazing scenes. Plus Shearer and Rob Lee (now of Derby) clashing heads. And all the goals flying in at our end, that day.

Signed in 1997 as a 21 year old, the great Irish international goalie amassed 462 appearances in his 12 seasons with the club, criminally departing for just £6 million to Man City in February 2009 when only 34 games from breaking NUFC's appearance record.

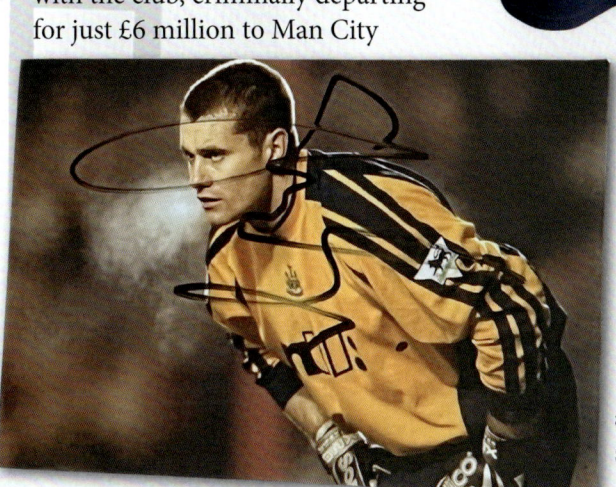

In my opinion, Shay was our greatest ever goalkeeper, a great shotstopper and so agile over such a sustained period.

66 ALAN SHEARER
2002/03 - Champions League

They called it the Champions League miracle... Bobby Robson's team qualified for the elite European competition after beating FK Željezničar Sarajevo 5-0 on aggregate in the third qualifying round.

In the first group stage we were drawn with Juventus, Dynamo Kiev and Feyenoord. After three straight defeats, we were left with a vertical uphill task. But then three straight wins (thanks to Bellamy's 90th-minute winner in Feyenoord) saw NUFC make history as the first side to progress from this position in Champions League history.

In the second group stage we twice beat Bayer Leverkusen and got a fantastic draw in the San Siro against Inter Milan; but three defeats overall unfortunately meant this remarkable story had to come to an end.

Personal memories include the car trip to Feyenoord and a base in Antwerp; the roof-mounted heater inside the away end in the Bayerarena and the pure bedlam in the San Siro when Shearer scored!

This is Alan Shearer's spare long-sleeved shirt, complete with star ball patch on the right sleeve, which was issued for the 2-1 victory over Dynamo Kiev at SJP on 29th October 2002.

67 GARY SPEED
2003/04 - Asia Cup

The 2003 FA Premier League Asia Cup was the first of these four-team pre-season tournaments to be held in the Bukit Jalil National Stadium in Kuala Lumpur. NUFC's opposition included Chelsea and Birmingham City, as well as our Malaysian hosts' national team.

This is the matchworn shirt that graced the back of Gary Speed in the tournament semi-final (aka our opening match) against Birmingham, which the lads won 2-1. Despite drawing against Chelsea in the grand final, the silverware eluded us as we went down, as usual, 5-4 in a penalty shootout.

Designed to fight the tropical heat, this Climacool shirt was equipped with Adidas 'dual-layer' technology, meaning that a thinner layer of fabric was sewn inside of the garment. As well as cooling you down, it supposedly also helped keep your muscles warm.

Photos from the Chelsea game show Speedo wearing the shirt with the dual layer intact.

The shirt was signed at a Sheffield United Supporters function in early 2011, whilst Speedo was managing the club.

68 GARY SPEED
2003/04 - Premier League

The long-sleeved grey third shirt matchworn by Gary Speed against Fulham on 21st October 2003.

The Adidas shirt has the 'dual layer' (inner vest) cut out on Speedo's request.

Construction work at Craven Cottage meant the game was played at QPR's Loftus Road, and the benefit of working in London that week ensured my attendance in the away end.

Unusually, we wore the grey shirt normally used in Europe against a Fulham side kitted out in their black away colours.

The match kick-off was delayed for 34 minutes, due to a suspect car parked nearby that was eventually dealt with by means of a controlled explosion.

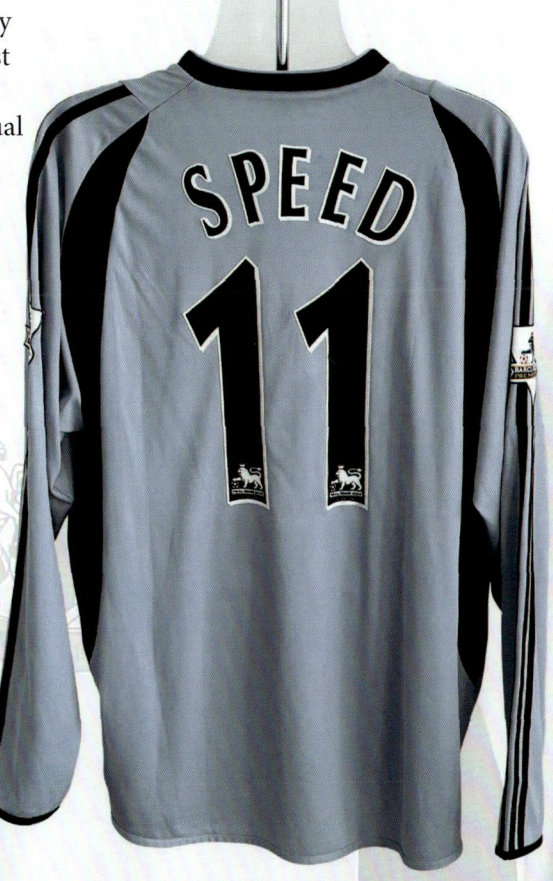

Fittingly, the match finally erupted into a marvellous passionate battle, NUFC typically 2-0 down within eight minutes, then turning it around to win 3-2.

Speedo spent six years at NUFC, making 285 appearances and scoring 40 goals. A true legend of the game and a natural leader. Tragically, he took his own life in November 2011, aged just 42.

69 **OLIVIER BERNARD**
2003/04 - UEFA Cup

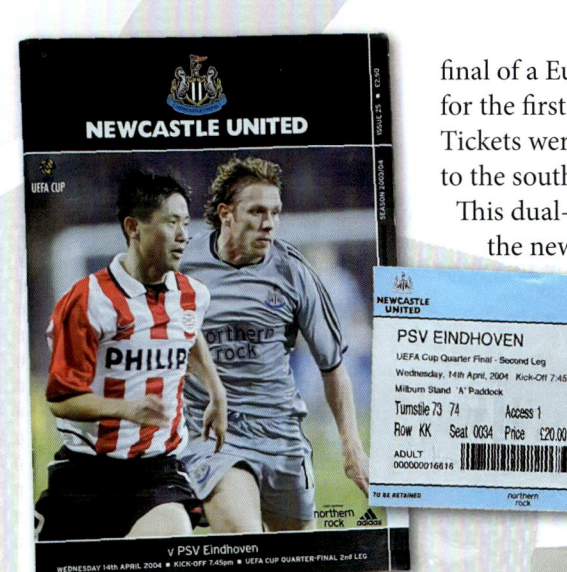

final of a European competition for the first time in 35 years. Tickets were immediately secured to the south of France!

This dual-layered shirt displayed the new sponsor Northern Rock, who took over the role in April 2003, remaining in place until their December 2011 sale to Virgin Money.

What a souvenir from the UEFA Cup quarter-final, second leg at St James' Park on 14th April 2004. That's when Newcastle beat PSV Eindhoven 2-1 in front of 50,083 fans.

Alan Shearer headed the lads in front after nine minutes when he powered home a near-post corner from Laurent Robert – only for PSV to level from the spot five minutes after half-time. But Gary Speed confirmed a last-four clash with Marseille by heading home another Robert corner after 66 minutes.

It put NUFC in the semi-

70 — ROBBIE ELLIOTT
2003/04 - UEFA Cup

Robbie Elliott's number three shirt, benchworn against Olympique Marseille in the UEFA Cup semi-final, second leg at the Stade Vélodrome on 6th May 2004. Sadly, two Didier Drogba goals gave Marseille a 2-0 win, meaning our UEFA Cup final trip to Gothenburg wasn't to be.

Even so, it was a great European run, this being the only match lost in 12 games. And it was a memorable trip, flying down to Nîmes for a couple of nights before driving down to Marseille on the day.

At the match, we were housed in a heavily fenced corner pen, the atmosphere throughout extremely full-on thanks to those insane Marseille Ultras. Even the walk back to the car and the subsequent slow crawl through traffic was quite an experience.

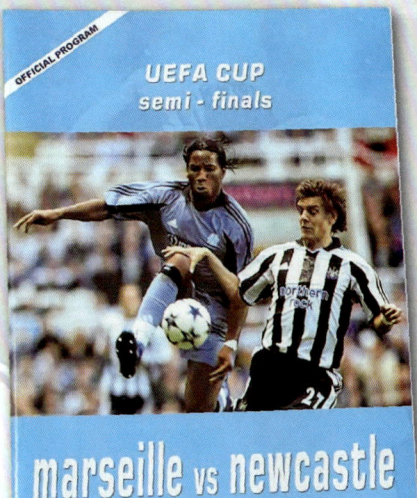

The Adidas 'Mundial' shirt design was consistent with those of a few other teams that were part of the manufacturers' club roster at the time. It features a transfer material badge and Adidas logo, printed size label and a Climacool logo to the lower front.

ALAN SHEARER
2005/06 - Alan Shearer Testimonial

'Shearer 9s' to family and friends.
It was a night long to be remembered by the 52,275 present, and the source of a great financial bonus to many good causes.

Having scored and succumbed

One of the rare player-issued shirt and shorts sets from Alan Shearer's testimonial vs Celtic on 11th May 2006.

The Newcastle side wore a 2005/06 issue home kit, with commemorative lettering on the front and non-standard shirt numbers. Each of the shirts was numbered 1-100 on the front – this is 51 – some being issued to players in the match, others to players who didn't eventually make it (I also have Michael Owens' number 10 from his own personal collection – numbered 87) and many other

to injury in the 4-1 derby win at Sunderland in April, Alan's final season had come to a premature end. Nevertheless, he came on here to score a penalty with the final kick of the match as Newcastle beat Celtic 3-2.

72 ANTOINE SIBIERSKI
2006/07 - UEFA Cup

Matchworn by Antoine Sibierski during the UEFA campaign of '06/07, this shirt featured the awesome World Cup 2006 Adidas numbering on the reverse and stylish, pointy heat-pressed stripes on the arms.

NUFC signed Sibierski from Manchester City on 31st August 2006. Many fans at the time were underwhelmed with the signing on a one-year contract, but his goalscoring form proved doubters wrong. In Europe, he made seven appearances and scored four essential goals against Levadia Tallinn, Fenerbahçe, Celta Vigo and Zulte-Waregem.

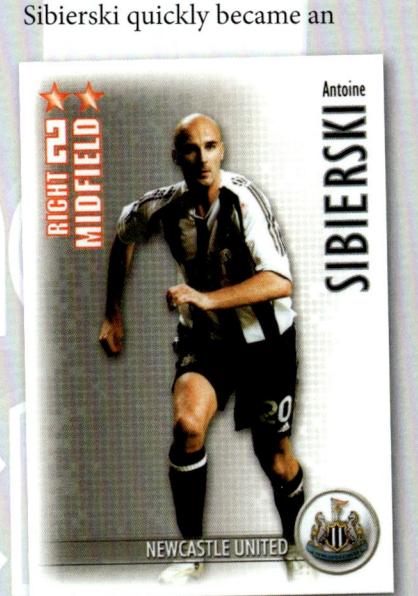

Sibierski quickly became an important member of the first team under Glenn Roeder, was loved by the fans, and ended up a true cult hero, making 39 appearances and scoring eight goals overall.

Many years later, whilst being interviewed, he had a message for any player struggling to cope with life at NUFC: "Put your heart and soul into it and the Toon Army will never forget you."

Spot-on, as ever. Thanks again for the memories, Sib.

73 **EMRE BELOZOGLU**
2006/07 - UEFA Cup

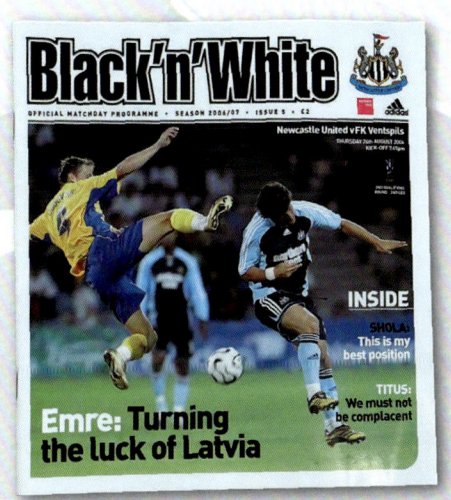

This black and blue away shirt was an Adidas template called 'Teamgeist' ('team spirit'), featuring a neckline that sits high around the back, with a rounded front. It has three stripes on the sleeves, interrupted by the UEFA Cup patch and Teamgeist logo, while pinstripes run right through the shirt. Again, I love the retro/futuristic style of the Adidas World Cup 2006 numbering and typography on the reverse.

This shirt was worn in Europe by the supremely gifted Turkish midfielder Emre Belözoğlu. It could have featured in any of the UEFA Cup away ties, against FK Ventspils, Levadia Tallinn, Palermo, and/or AZ Alkmaar.

Emre arrived from Inter Milan in the summer of 2005, at a cost of £4 million. He was small in stature but combative, with a sublime left foot and immense technical ability. His best moment was in the Tyne-Wear derby against Sunderland in October 2005, delivering a sharp corner that found Shola Ameobi to open the scoring, before acing a brilliant free-kick to win the game 3-2. He made 82 appearances, scoring six goals across his three seasons with the club.

74 ANDY CARROLL
2008/09 - Premier League

Gateshead lad Andy Carroll's matchworn shirt from the 2008/09 season.

Andy made his first-team debut in a 1-0 UEFA Cup win over Palermo on 2nd November 2006. At the deceptively tender age of 17 years and 300 days, the 6'4" striker became the youngest ever player to represent NUFC in Europe.

He scored his first competitive goal on his first home start, with a header (what else?) in a 2-2 draw against West Ham on 10th January 2009. He was wearing a long-sleeved number 39 just like this. It could even be the very one.

After 33 goals in 91 appearances, and helping NUFC to the Championship title in 2009/10, it was sad to see Andy leave for Liverpool in 2011. Our hero returned in 2019 for a second spell, but we only saw one more goal from him in 43 games.

Adidas 'ForMotion' shirts use a range of different fabrics in specific body locations 'to control and enhance muscle activity', and sculpted cuts and '3-D engineering' to maximise freedom of movement. Good news for the larger target man.

75 KEVIN NOLAN
2009/10 - Championship

scoring a memorable hat-trick. Kevin's matchworn shirt was gifted to an NUFC employee, who later kindly donated it to the cause.

A wreath was laid in a ceremony

Just as Sir Bobby Robson's life illuminated the beautiful game, a contest between his two former clubs provided a game fittingly full of vibrancy and colour to celebrate the life of our very own Geordie gentleman. Newcastle United beat Ipswich Town 4-0 on 26th September 2009, with Kevin Nolan

at the Sir Bobby statue. The game then got under way after a rendition of 'Abide with Me' and a minute's applause in his honour.

Both sides wore home colours, with additional embroidery for the occasion, along with the Sir Bobby Robson Foundation logo.

76 PETER LOVENKRANDS
2009/10 - FA Cup

"Peter Lovenkrands, Peter Lovenkrands. Signed him on a free, from Germany, Peter Lovenkrands..."

And here is the shirt that Peter wore in the FA Cup third round replay at SJP on 13th January 2010, when he scored a 'perfect treble'.

His celebration consisted of running towards the East Stand while tapping his left leg, slapping his head and then tapping his right foot – confirming he was aware of the significance of his hat-trick.

The shirt itself featured 'ForMotion' technology, with 3-D sculpted cuts of fabric that move naturally with the body for fit and comfort in motion. A fine touch was the debossed seahorses from the crest on the shirt bottom.

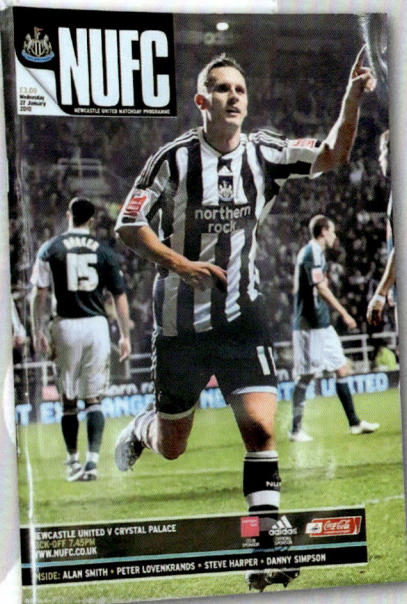

Danish international Lovenkrands was a fan favourite for three years, initially joining in January 2009 until the end of the relegation season, and then rejoining in August to score 16 goals in the 2009/10 Championship season.

Interestingly, Bobby Robson had wanted to sign Lovenkrands in 2000, when he was 20, but he headed to Rangers instead.

77 FITZ HALL
2009/10 - Championship

With the club's 15-year-long Adidas kit deal not quite at an end, the recent season-ending trend of previewing the new strip didn't happen in the final game against Ipswich Town on 24th April 2010. Instead, United wore the regular home replica shirts embellished with the embroidered text: 'Coca-Cola Championship Champions 2009/10'.

The game finished in a 2-2 draw, which gave NUFC the rare achievement of remaining undefeated at home in 25 League and cup matches throughout the whole season.

A great celebratory day was had by everyone at St James' Park. After the final whistle, the players then reappeared minus their shirts but clad in commemorative Adidas T-shirts with the motto 'Championship Winners 2009-10'.

The Coca-Cola Championship season had been great to watch, and an amazing adventure across the country. Overall, Newcastle amassed 102 points as the lads won 30 games, drew 12 and lost just four, scoring 90 goals in the process.

This shirt was match issued to Fitz Hall for the season's grand finale, though sadly the loanee from QPR didn't end up playing.

78 — **WAYNE ROUTLEDGE**
2009/10 - Championship

The infamous Adidas 'custard cream' shirt was unveiled in June 2009, beginning a memorable era for NUFC fans being forced to endure taunts from our rivals. Such was the backlash against the garish shirts, prices were slashed when they went on sale.

In truth, relegation made the timing all wrong for such an adventurous kit, though Adidas's Inigo Turner wasn't to know that when he created the shirt 18 months earlier.

It was "a bit of a Marmite shirt," the designer admitted to the *Evening Chronicle*. Having studied in Newcastle, he combined yellow shades from '70s and '90s away kits with traditional stripes to create a shirt "that was very much part of the DNA of the club," but with "a modern edge."

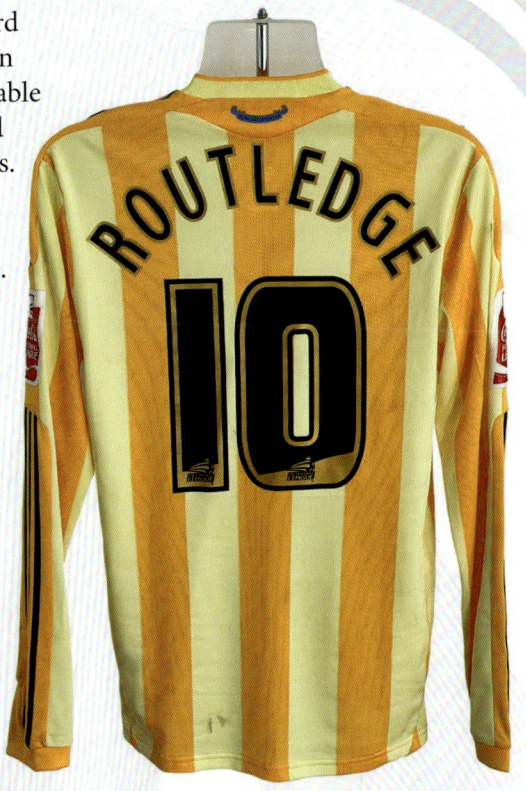

Needless to say, the season ended up a memorable one, and we wore the kit on 25 occasions during the Championship-winning season of 2009/10. And so the 'custard cream' ended up a big favourite with players and fans alike.

This specific shirt was worn by Wayne Routledge in the 3-2 win at Peterborough on 3rd April 2010, as Chris Hughton's side closed in on promotion.

79 XISCO
2010/11 - Premier League

Match issued and benchworn by Xisco against Fulham on 13th November 2010, this scoreless draw marked the first occasion that NUFC ever wore our usual home strip adorned with a poppy to commemorate the weekend of Remembrance Sunday.

This was Puma's first jersey for the club, featuring the famous black and white stripes, and incorporating the manufacturer's new three-point collar design first featured on the Italian World Cup shirt.

Francisco Jiménez Tejada was signed for £6 million in August 2008 and only made eleven appearances (seven as sub) before his contract was eventually terminated in 2013. He only scored once, on his debut, and was farmed out on loan many times in a largely forgettable stint with the club.

SHEFKI KUQI
2010/11 - Premier League

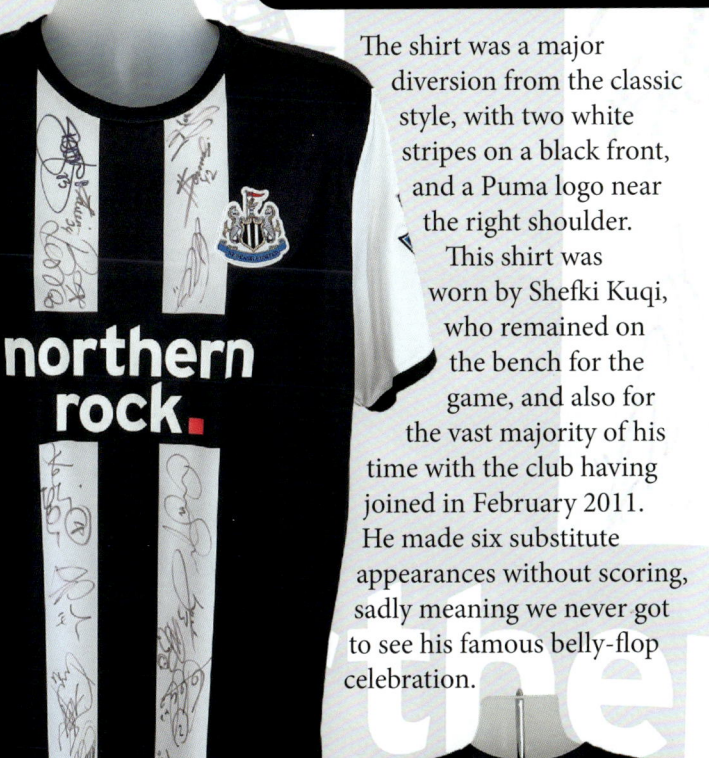

80

The shirt was a major diversion from the classic style, with two white stripes on a black front, and a Puma logo near the right shoulder.

This shirt was worn by Shefki Kuqi, who remained on the bench for the game, and also for the vast majority of his time with the club having joined in February 2011. He made six substitute appearances without scoring, sadly meaning we never got to see his famous belly-flop celebration.

NUFC premiered the next season's home shirt in the last game of the 2010/11 season against West Brom at St James' Park on 22nd May 2011. Typically, we let slip a 3-0 second-half lead (when we stood ninth in the Premier League table), allowing the visitors' Somen Tchoyi to score a hat-trick in 30 minutes, ensuring we were finally pegged back to 12th place.

81 CHEICK TIOTE
2011/12 - Premier League

Matchworn by Cheick Tioté in the 2-0 win over Bolton Wanderers at the Reebok Stadium on 26th December 2011. This was the last time that the Northern Rock sponsor appeared on the away shirt, shortly to be replaced by Virgin Money.

The shirt features two white diagonal stripes and the club crest in gold, while faint black stripes run diagonally in the opposite direction.

Cheick joined NUFC from FC Twente in August 2010 and spent almost seven years at St James' Park, making 156 appearances and scoring one memorable goal.

The hard-tackling Ivorian international midfielder trained exactly how he played – but off the pitch he was humble and somewhat shy, and rarely seen without a smile on his face.

Cheick sadly passed away aged just 30 in 2017 after collapsing during training with his last club side in Beijing, China.

He'll always live long in our hearts and be so fondly remembered for his stunning goal against Arsenal in February 2011.

82 DAVIDE SANTON
2011/12 - Premier League

On 1st January 2012, Virgin Money formally acquired Northern Rock from the UK Government and their logo was introduced on to the team's shirts – this after the bank had been nationalised in 2008 at the beginning of the global financial crisis.

The home match against Manchester United, three days later on 4th January, was the first to see the new sponsor, a temporary Virgin Money patch being hastily fastened over the old Northern Rock logo. Over the coming months the patch was fitted more securely and slowly became better finished-off, though it was still affixed over the old lettering.

As for the match itself, it was a cracker. This was the shirt worn by Davide Santon in the 3-0 hammering of the Red Devils in front of the Sky cameras. Demba Ba scored on the half-hour, Yohan Cabaye made it two straight after the break, and the hapless Phil Jones applied the final coffin nail in the 90th minute.

This season was to be one of the most memorable for some time, culminating in a fifth-place finish after some outstanding performances under Alan Pardew.

VURNON ANITA
2012/13 - Europa League

Matchworn in the first half of the second-leg game away to Metalist Kharkiv in the Europa League round of 32, this short-sleeved shirt proved to have an unpredictable destiny. It was jettisoned by Vurnon Anita at half-time in favour of a long-sleeved version – Ukraine can be chilly in February – then later signed for yours truly.

It features Europa League and Respect sleeve patches along with distinctive name and number typography that was a great favourite of mine.

A nice guy was Vurnon, always generous in his gifting of shirts to many NUFC fans. He joined from Ajax in the summer of 2012 and made 155 appearances, scoring three goals. His best came in the Europa Cup at Club Brugge that November, which I was lucky to witness on a trip to glorious Bruges with the travelling Mags.

Quite Interestingly, Vurnon has recently switched from the Dutch international side to representing Curaçao… and he records rap music under the pseudonym 'JR'.

NILE RANGER
2012/13 - Europa League

The long-sleeved lemon-yellow shirt worn by Nile Ranger on his European debut against Bordeaux in the Europa League group stage on 6th December 2012. We lost the match 2-0 at the Stade Chaban Delmas.

The asymmetrical shoulder panel was a major feature of this Puma shirt. Europa League player shirts didn't have the '1892' on the back of the neck like the Premier League versions.

Great memories of the trip to France include the long drive down to Gatwick from the North East and the flight over. Bordeaux was a charming city which we fully sampled day and night. The only downside to the whole excursion was a forgettable performance by the team when it really mattered.

After a promising start in the academy and reserves, London-born striker Ranger broke through into the first team. He signed a new five-and-a-half-year deal at the end of 2010, but loan spells at Barnsley and Sheff Wed followed, and he left in March 2013 with just two League goals to his name.

85 GABRIEL OBERTAN
2013/14 - Members' Shirt

Puma literature described the 2013/14 shirt as being inspired by the sports lifestyle brand's Spirit product line, featuring dryCell technology for enhanced performance, dragging moisture away from the body, improving air flow and keeping the body at the ultimate performance temperature.

That said, this unfamiliar half-and-half style was never worn competitively, despite being introduced on the club website as as the 'new members' home kit', a fourth different kit for the season.

This shirt was matchworn by 87th-minute sub Gabriel Obertan in the pre-season friendly 1-1 draw against the Portuguese side SC Braga on 10th August 2013.

By this time Wonga, a controversial, short-term loan company, had been installed as NUFC's primary sponsor, much to everyone's disappointment.

VURNON ANITA
2014/15 - Premier League

86

Anita came on as sub in the 63rd minute. It was an awful game that saw two NUFC players sent off, resulting in a 3-0 defeat. Although emotions were high and frustrations clearly evident post match, Vurnon kept his word and handed me his shirt. One other positive note was a great night out in Leicester afterwards, this being a major feature of following Newcastle away over many years, where the night out has often been better than the match itself!

NUFC matchworn shirts this season featured Power Active technology – offering 'muscle support and a moisture management system to stay cool and dry' – not to mention dryCell technology too, along with tipping on the sleeves and 'NUFC' lettering on the upper-back neck.

This shirt was worn by Vurnon Anita against Leicester at the King Power Stadium on 2nd May 2015.

171

87 **FABRICIO COLOCCINI**
2015/16 - Premier League

NUFC actually unveiled their new kit for the 2015/16 season in May 2015. However, in their haste to launch the new strip before the end of the 2014/15 season, a rather serious error was made.

Manufactured by Puma, the strip features the traditional black and white stripes of the club with blue trim around the collar and arms, and PWR ACTV athletic taping.

The unforeseen problem arose just hours before the club were due to showcase the new strip during the final game of the season at home to West Ham – when sponsors Wonga themselves unveiled a new corporate logo.

The change by the money-lending company meant there was no time for the new branding to feature on the kit. And with thousands of replica shirts already made, the new Newcastle shirts had to carry the old branding due to the production schedule.

This poppy shirt was matchworn by Fabricio Coloccini in the Stoke City game at St James' Park on 31st October 2015, a 0-0 draw. Colo was with the club for eight years from 2008-16, and was the North East Football Writers' Association Player of the Year for 2011.

88 ALEKSANDAR MITROVIC
2015/16 - Premier League

Mitro's matchworn poppy shirt from the Bournemouth game at the Vitality Stadium on 7th November 2015, where we ran out 1-0 winners.

Just for the record, the shirt featured Puma's new HeiQ fabric and ACTV taping technology, which was claimed to 'micro-massage specific areas, enabling a faster and more effective energy supply to the muscles'.

The '90s-inspired graphic on the shirt offered a different look to the clean lines of the home and third shirts, and paid homage to the attacking philosophy of the 'Entertainers' era, when we achieved our best ever Premier League finish.

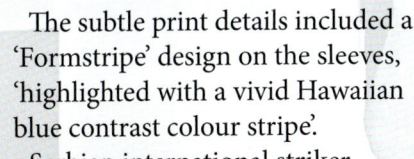

The subtle print details included a 'Formstripe' design on the sleeves, 'highlighted with a vivid Hawaiian blue contrast colour stripe'.

Serbian international striker Mitrovic arrived in Newcastle with a £13 million reputation from Anderlecht in 2015. He was booked after 22 seconds on his debut and was sent off in his second match. By the time he moved on to Championship Fulham in 2018 he had scored 17 goals in 72 games.

89 PAUL DUMMETT
2016/17 - Championship

Local Newcastle stopper Paul Dummett's matchworn shirt from the Wigan home match at St James' Park on 1st April 2017. We won 2-1, no kidding.

With NUFC newly relegated to the Championship after Steve McLaren's sacking in March, we were relying on Rafa Benitez for a quick return to the big league.

But let's not forget the part played by good old Puma and their ever-imaginative marketing department, who followed up last season's temporary technological glitch by "making waves of innovation." Somehow, Puma managed to "transform their shirts into high-performance equipment built to improve the capabilities of the players that wear them," reported Soccer.com. It was all to do with the "figure-hugging form"; the ACTV tape lining that gripped "on to the wearer's skin... sitting flush against key stability muscles in your upper back, lumbar, upper ribcage and lateral obliques."

And it worked like a dream!

In a tense race with Brighton, Rafa's lads only went and won the Championship title in dramatic fashion on the last day of the season – to return triumphantly to the Premier League for their 125th anniversary season.

90 DARRYL MURPHY
2016/17 - Championship

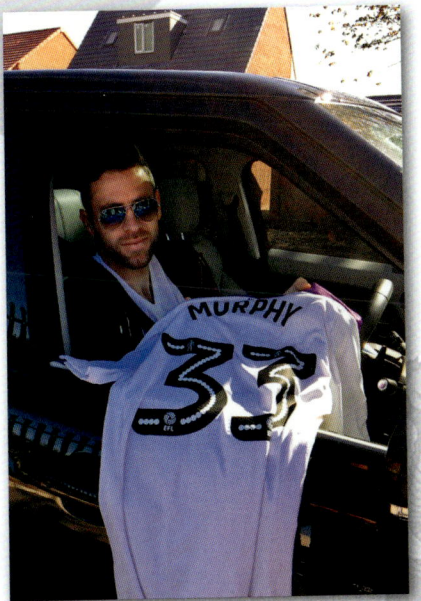

Darryl Murphy's matchworn away shirt from the Cardiff game on 28th April 2017. Newcastle won 2-0, with second-half goals by Christian Atsu and Isaac Hayden.

The ACTV shirt was again worn, this time in the third colours of white and purple.

The fact that promotion had already been achieved, and that the game was switched to Friday night for live TV, meant that some folks opted not to make the trek to the Principality.

Those that did make the effort included three of us who overcame the daunting journey to enjoy a cracking trip. When Darryl handed me his shirt after the game, it made the night even more precious than I could have imagined. Another great memory came later when my friend was asked for ID to gain entry to a bar in Cardiff. He was 52 at the time.

Darryl was an unusual signing for NUFC in that he was 33 years of age. Good job he didn't go out for refreshments with us in Cardiff. Brought in to do a specific job, he scored six goals in 18 appearances in his solitary season on Tyneside.

91 JAMAAL LASCELLES
2017/18 - Premier League

NUFC celebrated its 125th anniversary during the 2017/18 season, and a special commemorative version of the crest was commissioned, with shining gold and silver highlights to signify the milestone.

FUN88, the Far Eastern gaming company, became the primary partner as part of an initial three-year agreement.

This shirt was worn by captain Jamaal Lascelles in the 3-0 drubbing of West Ham at St James' Park on 26th August 2017. For the first few games of the season PL badges were worn, before the appearance of a sleeve sponsor.

For the first time in 25 years the new home jersey featured contrasting red numbers, a great tradition dating back to the 1939/40 season. Due to issues with legibility, the club switched to red numbers on a white background in the 1950s through to 1992/93 – although in 1975/76 and from 1981-87 the numbers were again just imposed, not very successfully, directly over the stripes.

92 | MO DIAME
2017/18 - Premier League

This is the shirt worn by Senegal international midfielder Mo Diamé away at Burnley on Monday 30th October 2017, a game we lost 1-0 to a goal by future Magpie Jeff Hendrick.

For this Remembrance Day match, NUFC.com reported, "Both teams wore custom shirts with the poppy motif added. A pre-game tribute saw both teams cluster round the centre circle while representatives of the Armed Forces lined up at pitchside for a rendition of 'The Last Post'."

Half-time guest at Turf Moor was Geoff Nulty, an underrated player for both sides back in the 1970s.

Mo handed me his shirt as he got on to the team bus after the match. Personally, I think he must be one of the nicest footballers you could ever meet, kind and generous in giving shirts to many fans that I know. A very pleasant man, and another example of an unsung fans' hero in his three seasons with Newcastle United, where he made 103 appearances.

Mo wore number 15 in his Championship-winning season with the club, and number ten in the Premier League.

93 ISAAC HAYDEN
2018/19 - Premier League

This season, NUFC unveiled a new brand identity to link all of the club's work in the fields of diversity, inclusion and welfare.

'United As One' was symbolised by a new 'black and white solidarity ribbon' (or a 'scarf' as it's commonly known), proudly worn by players during the Premier League clash with Southampton at St James' Park on 20th April 2019. On the day, the new logo was visible everywhere, including posters, the stadium big screen and advertising boards, and on a specially commissioned banner display at the Gallowgate End by Wor Flags.

The club's work towards ending discrimination and inequality in football and in society has involved LGBT and disabled supporter groups, and initiatives such as On the Ball, Be A Game Changer and Memory Café.

The players' ribboned shirts were later auctioned to raise money for community projects – and I was lucky enough to win the shirt worn by Isaac Hayden in the 3-1 victory.

It's strange to note that the Newcastle shirts had no sleeve sponsorship this season, moving back to featuring a Premier League patch on each arm.

94 ANTONIO BARRECA
2018/19 - Premier League

Matchworn against Tottenham Hotspur on 2nd February 2019 at Wembley Stadium, this is one Newcastle United kit that's definitely far more memorable than the player wearing it that day.

Launched under #TheFabricOfNewcastle banner, the shirt was a contemporary take on the Magpies' iconic change strip worn during the 1995/96 season. Here, the maroon and blue hoops featured EvoKNIT technology, adorned with a gold club crest and FUN88 branding.

In my opinion this was an awesome modern twist on the great 1995/96 shirt. Personal memories of the kit include Salomón Rondón's swashbuckling performance at Huddersfield, and the last goal scored by him in the 4-0 thrashing of Fulham at Craven Cottage in May 2019 – this following a memorable few days in the capital which culminated in a momentous trip to the match, with six boatloads of fellow Mags tearing up the Thames on a booze cruise.

As for Antonio Barreca, he came on in the 86th minute in the 1-0 defeat to Spurs, only ever playing a little over four minutes in his loan career with NUFC.

95 | MARTIN DUBRAVKA
2018/19 - Premier League

ultimate ergonomic fit to maximise an individual's performance when in competition and ensure sportswear doesn't hinder their output'.

Dúbravka signed initially on loan on transfer deadline day in January 2018, and then permanently in summer 2018. Ever-present during the 2018/19 Premier League season, in February 2019 he was recognised as the 2018 Player of the Year by the North East Football Writers' Association.

Poppy Day charity shirt worn by Martin in the 2-1 home win against Bournemouth at St James' Park on 10th November 2018. The shirt is signed on front and back.

This is a very tight-fitting goalkeeper shirt based on the standard Puma template worn during the 2018 World Cup and the 2018/19 season. This version was part of the all-purple goalies' second kit (Bournemouth wore light green), with a mechanical pattern stretching across the chest and stomach.

Additional features include the poppy transfer, the club badge and the lightweight, ventilated material sold as EvoKNIT technology. According to Puma, this is 'the

189

96 JONJO SHELVEY
2019/20 - Asia Cup

The 2019/20 season marked the 50th anniversary of Newcastle winning the Inter-City Fairs Cup, the last major silverware lifted by the team. The kit introduced to mark the occasion featured a distinctly stylish monochromatic crest.

This was Newcastle's second appearance in the Asian Trophy in China, having taken part in the inaugural event in Malaysia back in 2003. Jonjo Shelvey's shirt was matchworn in the 4-0 defeat to Wolves on Wednesday 17th July 2019 and the 1-0 victory over West Ham three days later. These games took place in the Nanjing Olympic Sports Centre Stadium and Shanghai's Hongkou Stadium.

Restrictions in China on the display of gaming adverts saw NUFC wear shirts with alternative sponsors, swapping FUN88 for the Chinese app National Sports, with sleeve sponsorship from Northumbria University also evident. There was some speculation around the red, white and blue app logo, but in fact it was nothing to do with Sports Direct.

Our win against West Ham secured third place, having earlier lost 4-1 to eventual winners Manchester City.

97 | NUMBER 8 - BLM & NHS
2019/20 - Premier League

Strict admission protocols laid down by the Premier League permitted a total of just 300 people inside the stadium for this pandemic-hit home match against Sheffield United on 21st June 2020.

Playing behind closed doors was simply unprecedented for Newcastle United. Even in that meagre crowd, only 105 were allowed in and around the pitch, including players, coaches, officials and medical staff.

Even in these strange Covid-affected circumstances, the lads managed to beat the Blades 3-0, and this is the shirt worn in the match by Jonjo Shelvey.

Players from both sides wore shirts with 'Love the NHS' heart-shaped logos, and the motto 'Black Lives Matter' appeared above their number in place of their name. BLM sleeve logos were also displayed by both Newcastle United and Sheffield United teams. United against racism.

What was termed as 'a moment's silence' was staged before kick-off in honour of all those affected by the pandemic.

98 | JONJO SHELVEY
2020/21 - League Cup

Jonjo's matchworn shirt from the fourth-round Carabao Cup tie at Newport on 30th September 2020. The match ended 1-1, Jonjo having equalised in the 87th minute with a wonderful curling shot. And then we went on to win 5-4 on pens – only the second victory in 12 competitive shootout attempts!

Played behind closed doors, the evening match was Newcastle United's first at Rodney Parade, and also our first win in Newport, having lost 4-2 on our only previous visit, at Somerton Park in 1947 – which of course was the away match to the record-breaking 13-0 home win.

NUFC's 2020/21 home kit was the last made by Puma after they had reportedly signed a short-term extension to produce the kit for one last season. Using dryCELL technology, they created a design with thinner stripes than in other recent seasons, maintaining a classic NUFC look.

The shirt worn by Jonjo that night had the Carabao sleeve patch on the right arm, while the left sleeve patch was from the partnership with global investment house ICM.com.

99 | JONJO SHELVEY
2020/21 - Premier League

The 2020/21 third kit is an eye-catching 'prism violet' design, featuring a bold pattern based on the steelwork of Newcastle's number one historic landmark, the Tyne Bridge.

It is completed in fine style with a club crest and sponsor branding in the same 'fizzy yellow' accent colour as the contemporary away kit.

This is one of my favourite ever NUFC away shirts. I love the way the yellow tone of the badges, sponsor, player name and numbering contrast with the purple and black. A wonderful shirt from Puma.

Jonjo Shelvey's number eight shirt was matchworn away at Tottenham Hotspur's new stadium on 27th September 2020.

Sadly, as the match was played behind closed doors, there were no Newcastle fans present to cheer the 1-1 draw secured extremely late on by Steve Bruce's men.

After a VAR check in the 97th minute, a penalty kick was awarded and Callum Wilson did the business from the spot, blasting the ball low, just inside the left post.

197

KARL DARLOW
2020/21 - Premier League

The full evolution of goalkeeper shirt design started in this book with a plain green goalkeeper shirt in 1980 and ends with this awesome bright pink creation in 2020.

This keeper's away shirt featured a hexagonal pattern coupled with gradient shading. The same 'TeamFinal21' Puma template was used on all three NUFC goalkeeper shirts this season – the dark turquoise home version, the neon-pink away shirt and the bright yellow third option from the same 'marker-pen' colour palette. All three outfits' shorts and socks matched the shirts.

This shirt was worn by Karl during the course of the 2020/21 season, and was purchased via the Newcastle United Foundation's end-of-season online auctions, where shirts are donated by the first-team squad to raise significant funds for the community, education, employability, sports, and health & wellbeing programmes delivered by the Foundation across the North East.

199

101 RYAN FRASER
2021/22 - Premier League

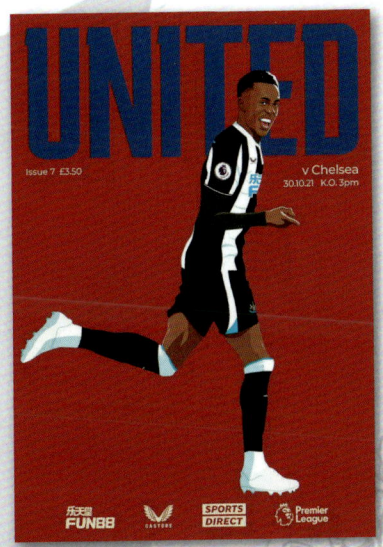

the home match against Chelsea on 30th October 2021 – shortly after the completion of a takeover by a consortium consisting of PCP Capital Partners, Reuben Brothers and the Public Investment Fund of Saudi Arabia (PIF). There's so much promise for the future now!

"Who's that team we call United?
Who's that team we all adore?
Oh, we play in Black and White,
And we all know how to fight,
We'll support you ever more…"

The first NUFC offering from British sportswear manufacturer J Carter Sporting Club Ltd (aka Castore) was a retro-inspired shirt with a mandarin collar, referencing the classic from the '90s 'Entertainers' era.

The new design featured a black stripe down the shirt's centre, wider white stripes either side and large black side panels, with light blue accents beneath the collar buttons and across the back to compliment the colour of the scroll on the club crest. As a nod to the club's supporters, the words 'Black and White Army' adorn the inside of the collar.

This poppy shirt was worn in

Author

Gavin Haigh's life as a passionate NUFC shirt collector began as a seven-year-old in June 1976 with a trip with his mother to Stan Seymour's sports shop in the centre of Newcastle. He attended his first match in October 1976, standing on the Gallowgate, became a Milburn Stand season-ticket holder in 1992 and continues to attend every home match, his love and commitment to the club never wavering. Gavin's knowledge of the history of the club and their shirts is second to none, his NUFC shirt collection currently standing at close to 1000, of which 275 are matchworn shirts.

Acknowledgements

Writing this book has been a personal labour of love that I could never have completed without the support of an equally passionate network of friends and family.

Thanks to my wife Lynn for her love and support, and for acting as a sounding board on this project; to legendary shirt collector Simon Shakeshaft for his inspirational advice and encouragement; to NUFC shirt-collector friends Andy Wardman, Stuart Cumings and Ollie Holst for their constant help; and to Alan Golightly, Mike Bolam, Marc Corby and Bobby Kelters for their continued backing and support.

Thanks also to Dave Mann for his friendship and guidance; and to Gary and Derek at Conker Editions for their help in realising my vision.

I would like to personally express my gratitude to the countless other friends, shirt collectors and enthusiasts who have helped with advice or with items for the collection; also to the Fairs Club, who allowed my nostalgic memories to flourish whilst meeting club legends. You have all contributed to making the creation of this book such a positive experience.

Finally, special thanks to the many Newcastle players who have gone the extra mile on my behalf; to David Kelly and Darren Peacock; to Uncle Billy; to my daughters, Lauren and Georgia, who donned the NUFC kit so many times during their early years, and once again to my wonderful late mother and father.

Teamwork...
many thanks to all our supporters...

Stuart Cumings | Iain Hood | David Pallister | Paul Lyon
Jim Rowntree | Marc Corby | Steven Westlake | Stephen Cross
Matthew Ketchell | Darren Storey | Mark 'JamJar' Wilkinson
Adam Crooks | Paul Wardle | Jon Elliott | Nick Fail
Jonny Henderson | Keith Burn | Adam Taylor
Ross Morecroft | David Coulson | Retro NUFC | Alan Golightly
Kevin Golightly | Martin Golightly | Paul Town | Ollie Holst
Ian Reay | Rich Johnson - Football Attic | Nathan Rauscher
Steve Kelters | Paul Tyson | Clayton Foston | Andy Barr
Gary Turner | Andrew Scott | Gerard Cantwell | Stephen Street
Jez #ErasureSmile | Kenny McLachlan | Trevor Smith
Peter Whitney | Andy Bird | Rafal Charzynski | Philip Marriott
David Low | Les Ruffell | Chris Watson | David Simm
Michael Martin | Andrew Freckleton | Danny Montgomery
Mark Dawson | Caroline Murray | Chris Taylor
Ian Symington | Neil Sproates | Garry Laverty
Hakeem Ajibola | Stephen Vernon-Clarke
Peter Todd | Ollie Holmes | Phil Jobson
Biffa - NUFC.com | Nigel Maddison
Paul Saint | Keith Wilson | John Rayner
George Middleton | David Thompson
Carles Mir | Stephen Nelson
Peter Nelson | Michael Coates
Michael Douglas | Eric Hogg
Grant Appleyard | Lesley Hutchinson
Terje Kvicksson | Keith Mason
Gordon & Fizzy | Helen Bott
Laris Lim | Andy Robinson

Paul Anderson | Brian Neilson | Dan King | Neal Heard
David Todd | Paul Young | Angus Monro | Ross Monro
Noel Monro | Ben Monro | Anthony Brydon | Terence Casson
Joanne & Chloe Graham | Paul Marshall | Stephen Robinson
Gavin Hope @Kit_Geek | Nidzam Kamaruddin | Jack Bowie
Andrew Whitehill | Gary Oliver | John Wardle | Steve Curry
Chris Gates | Tara & Dan Devlin | Bill Ord | Kelly Ord
Robert Young | Daniel Wardle | Arthur Preston
Chris Biskupek | Stephen Gapik | Neil Reay | Dave Mann
Ian Bates | David Mankelow | Nat & Darcey Mankelow
Mick Lapsley | Andy McClay | Russell Osborne | David Walker
Paul Lazenby | Kris Leighton | Barry Guttridge | Steve Brooks
Bobby Kelters | Paul McKenzie | Josh Evans | David Maughan
Michael Murray | David Usher | Jared Robinson | Mark Allison
Mark McCarthy | Dave Horne | Kallebe Gerais | Ian Gaskin
Lee Hermitage | Alan Parke | Barry Rojack | Anthony Sedgwick
Ingo Wolters | Anthony Taylor | Ian Pringle – Ips
Colin McKee | Martin Trinder | Jack Terry
Jason Fairless | Jeff Rippon | Luca Welsh
Barbara Fox | John 'Leazes Jack' Robson
Alan Bye | Mark & Matty Batey
Nigel Williams | Julie Hall
David Turnbull | Mary McKay
Owen Dodd | Dean Christopher
Carol Christopher
Jasmine Christopher
Ben Freeman | Jamie Thompson
Barry Thomas-Brown | Ben Turner
Darren Curry | Neil Davenport
Andrew Rutherford | Jane White
Tony Sealey | Neil Smith
Ian Brown | Jody Moore

Rob Stokes | Paul Lamb | Mike Rennie | Andrew Ward
Matthew Ward | Brian Ballentine | Malcolm McDougall
Tony, Marcus & Sean - NUFC Forever | Alec Irving | Alex Evans
Dunil Baines | Mark Oselton | Paul Kniveton | Stephen Clark
Ian Cameron | Michael Stephenson | Gavin Webster | Paul White
Andrew Webster | Jackie Harrisson | Jonathan Edwards
Paul Heighes | Mark Huddart | Paul Smith | Andrew Wardman
Claire Whitehill | Gerry Baines | Ronnie | Malcolm Colledge
Jesse Rabbeljee | Pete Weller | Colin Varty | Darren Hann
Angie Stanger-Leathes | Anthony Britton | Michael Clifford
John Bradley | Kong Kiat Kan | Zheng Yan Sheng | Stephen Best
Nigel Forde | Matthew Faria - Boston Mag | Rodney Hudspith
Geoffrey Hutchinson | Martin Wilkinson | Johnny Gavin
William Curran | Derek Richardson - The Fairs Club
Les Motherby - The Football Kit Podcast | Chris Nicholson
Cal Muir FYD | Francisco Tello | Alan Morland
Anthony Raine | Doug Boyle | Geoff Clarkson
Luke Anderson | Harry Elliott | Sean Quinn
Craig & Ben Chadwick | Rob Yorke
Craig Stoddart | Jonathan Auty
Steve Caithness | Luke Reynolds
Jonathan Pickett | David Henson
Mark Pearce | Neil Bramfitt
John Devlin | Joe Staines
The Kirkliston Browns
Aiden Renno | Branden Renno
Denis Hurley | Adam Morland
Mike Stowe | Lewis Salisbury
David Greaves | Kevin Douglas
Mark Husband | Jim Bishop
Andre Martin-Comrie
Dave Scott | Roger Douglass